Sally M. Walker

WRITTEN IN BONE

Buried Lives
of Jamestown
and Colonial
Maryland

 Carolrhoda Books Minneapolis · New York

For all who understand the importance of asking questions and especially for those who enjoy embarking on a voyage of discovery. Knowledge truly is the key that opens all doors.

—*S.M.W.*

Texture fills the title type on the cover, the title page, and the chapter headings and is also used in the background of the title page. The pattern is an extreme close-up of the skull of a woman who lived in colonial Maryland. The texture thus is literally "written in bone."

Front Cover: Skeleton of Levy Neck boy in situ. *Back Cover:* Archaeologists document the graves at the site of the Catholic chapel in St. Mary's City.

Carolrhoda Books
A division of Lerner Publishing Group, Inc.
241 First Avenue North
Minneapolis, MN 55401 U.S.A.

Website address: www.lernerbooks.com

Library of Congress Cataloging-in-Publication Data

Walker, Sally M.
    Written in bone : buried lives of Jamestown and Colonial Maryland / by Sally M. Walker.
        p.   cm.
    ISBN: 978-0-8225-7135-3 (lib. bdg. : alk. paper)
    ISBN: 978-0-7613-8107-5 (eBook)
    1. Forensic anthropology—Juvenile literature. 2. Forensic osteology—Juvenile literature.
3. Human remains (Archaeology)—Virginia—Jamestown—Juvenile literature. 4. Human remains
(Archaeology)—Chesapeake Bay Region (Md. and Va.)—Juvenile literature. 5. Jamestown (Va.)—
Antiquities—Juvenile literature. 6. Chesapeake Bay Region (Md. and Va.)—Antiquities—Juvenile
literature. I. Title.
GN69.8.W35 2009
614'.17—dc22   2007010768

Manufactured in the United States of America
10 - PC - 9/1/13

CONTENTS

YEARS AGO, when I was in college, I studied archaeology, a branch of science that helps us learn about people of the past. My work included an excavation—what archaeologists call a dig—in which my classmates and I uncovered evidence of the lives of people who had lived several thousand years earlier. The only remaining traces of their civilization were darkened circles of soil, fire-cracked rock surrounded by charcoal, and stone artifacts: spearpoints, knives, and a pestle for grinding corn. I wondered: *Who were these people? How had they lived?*

Much more recently, while touring an eighteenth-century plantation in South Carolina, I saw a sign that directed visitors toward a cemetery where slaves had been buried. An overgrown path, obviously seldom used, led into the woods. I decided to visit the cemetery and pay my respects to the people who had built and worked on the plantation.

I soon reached a clearing scattered with saplings and shrubs. A small wooden sign noted that in keeping with African tradition, the graves were not marked. I looked around, wondering where they might be. Then I remembered that an archaeologist had once given me a hint that could answer my question. During the eighteenth century, people were usually buried in wooden coffins. Over time, as the wood weakens, the weight of the soil on the coffin's lid may cause it to collapse. The soil sinks, leaving a depression on the surface of the ground.

Looking at the ground more carefully, I noticed slivers of shadows, visible only when the sun's rays caught the edges of very slight indentations in the soil surface. And suddenly I could see a pattern of graves, side by side, one after another, reminders of the people who had lived and worked on the land around me. *Who were they, and what were their lives like?*

Those questions stayed with me, just as the questions of my college years had. Then Dr. Douglas Owsley (*pictured, facing page*), a scientist at the Smithsonian Institution, asked me if I would be interested in writing a book about colonial settlers who had lived during the seventeenth and eighteenth centuries in Virginia and Maryland. This area, called the Chesapeake because it surrounds the Chesapeake Bay, includes the settlement of Jamestown as well as many other settlements. I immediately agreed to write the book. The prospect was particularly exciting because I knew that Dr. Owsley learns about the people of the past in an unusual way:

he studies their skeletons. His specialty, forensic anthropology, has revealed details about the past that we might otherwise never have learned.

Graves are discovered every day. Some, like those found during archaeological excavations, may be expected. Others are completely unexpected. These graves–unmarked and long forgotten–are uncovered as land is used for new purposes, such as the construction of buildings and roads. Sometimes bones are exposed as water and wind erode soil from the land. Regardless of the manner in which a grave is uncovered, ethical scientists will open it and remove the contents only for a legitimate reason. Archaeologists follow certain procedures required by federal, state, and local laws. If a burial is in a known cemetery, the permission of a church or other religious authority may also be needed. In all cases, human remains must be handled in a manner that respects the dead as well as the customs of the living.

As part of my research for this book, I joined Dr. Owsley and his crew on a dig in Talbot County, Maryland (*right*). There we excavated the unmarked graves of twelve colonial settlers, buried nearly three hundred years ago. The remains we found included adults, a teenager, and infants.

Excavating a human skeleton is an affecting experience that can provoke many emotions. At first I worried that I might accidentally damage or break one of the bones with the edge of the trowel I was using to remove soil. Then I worried about my reaction to seeing the bones. Would they still have flesh on them? (Dr. Owsley explained that the soil conditions in the area made that highly unlikely.) Would I feel frightened? Might my stomach feel queasy?

When the first glimpses of bones appeared, my worries vanished. They were replaced with a sense of awe as I realized I was touching more than bones. I was touching a real person who had lived and then died several hundred years ago. An intense desire filled me, a desire to learn all I could about this individual's life and death and to treat these remains with respect.

One of the graves I helped to excavate contained the remains of an infant who had lived only five or six months. As the mother of two children, I felt sad when I saw the tiny bones. I thought of the baby's mother, possibly the last person to touch the child, and I sensed a connection with her that reached across hundreds of years. In a small way, our lives touched. Once again, I wondered: *Who were these people? What were their lives like?*

As I continued my research for this book, I asked the same questions about the first human inhabitants of the Chesapeake—Native Americans such as the Powhatan, who lived on land that later became part of Virginia, and the Yaocomaco, who made their home in the future colony of Maryland. I learned that the study of Indian remains is a subject of great controversy. For cultural and spiritual reasons, some people of Native American descent object to the removal of their ancestors' remains from burial sites for scientific study. In the United States, when scientists find remains that they determine to be Indian, the law generally requires that excavation, testing, and analysis stop. Native American officials must be contacted. They decide what will be done with the remains.

This book tells the story of past peoples through the analysis of their bones and graves. In recognition of the perspective of some Native Americans on this type of study, I've chosen to refrain from including photographs of Indian remains or graves. *Written in Bone* is therefore limited to the study of colonial burials. This choice is meant not to diminish the importance of Native Americans in the history of the Chesapeake region, but rather to respect the desire of their descendants to see their remains treated in a manner that respects their cultural customs.

Our investigations begin with a discovery dating to the early 1600s in Jamestown, Virginia. From there, we'll witness the excavation of graves that span more than a century of colonial history. We'll see how archaeologists, forensic anthropologists, and other scientists work together to answer questions like those I've continually found myself asking. Along with these explorers of the past, we'll visit lost settlements and hear untold stories, some of which are written only in bone.

—*Sally M. Walker*

Chapter One

A GRAVE MYSTERY

ON AUGUST 16, 2005, the air temperature on the bank of the James River in Jamestown, Virginia, hovered at 100°F (38°C). Sunlight flooded the beige-colored soil. At the bottom of a carefully excavated pit, the rounded surface of a human skull gleamed with a yellow brown luster. The teeth shone white against the darker jawbone and the brownish soil beneath. The skeleton's leg bones stretched long and straight, toward the end of the grave. In contrast, the arms were chaotically bent. The left arm lay across the body, with the right flung up toward the shoulder.

Who was this person? There was no gravestone to offer a name. No signs of a coffin, no pieces of clothing, no buttons. Nothing to identify the remains. Only bones.

Yet the small group of scientists who had gathered a few inches from the pit's rim were confident they were about to learn more. One of them,

Douglas Owsley, positioned himself next to the grave and studied the skeleton. He looked at the skull, particularly the teeth. Then he scrutinized the ends of each leg bone and arm bone. He examined the pelvis, the part of the skeleton formed by the bones of the hip and lower backbone. It didn't take him long to reach a conclusion. "He was about fifteen years old when he died. And he was European," Owsley told the others.

Puzzles of the Chesapeake

The scientists who found the boy's grave have spent years working at several extraordinary sites in the Chesapeake Bay region. This area includes the modern states of Virginia, Maryland, and Delaware. The Chesapeake is of special interest to people who study U.S. history because colonists built the first permanent English settlement in North America here more than four hundred years ago.

The lives and deaths of these settlers have long intrigued historians and scientists. Most early colonists could not read or write, so the historical record–a term used by historians to refer to documents written by people of the past–contains little information about them. Historians have read and reread the surviving written records from the colonies' earliest days. These materials contain fascinating information about the settlers and their adventures. But they don't tell the whole story.

Archaeologists try to fill in the gaps in the historical record. They study buildings and man-made objects, called artifacts, created by people who lived in the past. They also study the remains people have left behind. As they find, excavate, and analyze these objects–including skeletons–archaeologists help us understand the past more fully and reclaim the histories of individuals who had been forgotten with the passage of time.

The interpretation of skeletal remains is a specialized branch of science known as forensic anthropology. The word *forensic* refers to the use of science and technology to help provide evidence or facts in a court of law. Anthropology is the scientific study of human beings and their ancestors. A forensic anthropologist, then, is a specialist who examines skeletons for clues that will provide evidence about the life and death of the people to whom they belonged. The skills these scientists use to help solve crimes and provide evidence in court are also perfectly suited to the study of human remains of centuries past.

HISTORIANS AND ARCHAEOLOGISTS
had no idea who was buried in this grave (*facing page*) when it was discoverd at Jamestown in 2005.

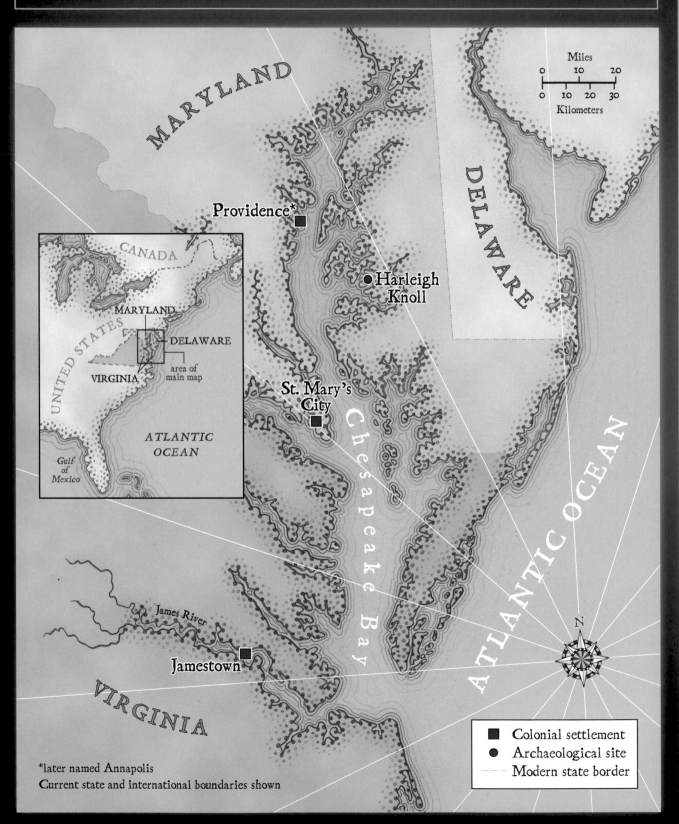

MAJOR ENGLISH SETTLEMENTS *in the* COLONIAL CHESAPEAKE REGION, 1650

MARYLAND

DELAWARE

Miles
0   10   20
0   10   20   30
Kilometers

Providence*

Harleigh Knoll

St. Mary's City

CANADA

MARYLAND

DELAWARE

UNITED STATES

VIRGINIA

area of main map

ATLANTIC OCEAN

Gulf of Mexico

Chesapeake Bay

ATLANTIC OCEAN

James River

N

Jamestown

VIRGINIA

■ Colonial settlement
● Archaeological site
---- Modern state border

*later named Annapolis
Current state and international boundaries shown

The tales told by colonial skeletons include sickness, sadness, and brain-teasing puzzles. Doug Owsley, one of the world's leading forensic anthropologists, is an expert at coaxing these stories from bones. He can determine through skeletal studies whether a person was old or young, healthy or sickly. He can usually tell if the bones belonged to a male or a female. Had he or she done hard physical labor? Owsley can often find out. Sometimes, the bones even tell him the exact cause of death.

The grave of the teenage boy whom Owsley examined was among more than thirty discovered inside James Fort, in Jamestown, Virginia. The fort's history dates to early 1607, when a group of men and boys arrived from England in three ships. They and their sponsor, the Virginia Company of London, shared the same goal: to get rich. They hoped that the lands surrounding the Chesapeake Bay would hold great wealth, especially silver and gold.

During the summer of 1607, the settlers built the fort and named their new settlement Jamestown, in honor of the English king, James I. Although the fort burned down in January 1608, by April of that year the men had replaced it with another. They also built houses, a church, and storage buildings inside the fort's walls.

More colonists journeyed on ships from England, including the first English women in 1608. The year 1619 saw the arrival of the first people from Africa, who came to Jamestown unwillingly. Initially, these Africans had been taken forcibly from their homeland and held captive on a Portuguese slave ship. The captain of a privateer—a privately owned

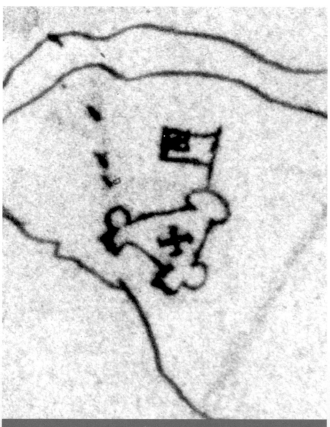

PEDRO DE ZUÑIGA was Spain's ambassador to England in the early 1600s. He sent the king of Spain reports and maps—including a map of James Fort (*above*) dating from 1609—that confirmed England's efforts to populate and protect its new colony of Virginia. This crude drawing gave researchers clues about what shape the original fort may have had.

ship that captures another ship and claims its cargo—took fifty to sixty of the Africans from the slave ship. About twenty of these people were taken to Jamestown. The historical record is unclear as to whether they lived out their lives as slaves or became free persons.

Together, the people of Jamestown built more homes and government buildings, grew crops, operated businesses, raised families, and buried their dead. In their quest for land and riches, the settlers spread out into other areas of the Virginia colony and built plantations. (In the seventeenth century, the word *plantation* meant "farm.") Jamestown quickly outgrew the area of James Fort. The materials used in the fort's construction were removed and used for other building projects. By the time the historical record reaches the 1630s, all mention of James Fort is gone.

A PHOTOGRAPH TAKEN in 1852 shows a cart in front of the old church tower that marked the location of the Jamestown settlement. Most historians assumed that James Fort, which had been built nearby, had washed away.

Finding the Fort

For many years, the crumbling brick tower of a seventeenth-century church stood as the only readily visible remains of the Jamestown settlement. During the late 1890s, a group of women founded an organization, the Association for the Preservation of Virginia Antiquities, to protect the church ruins. Although the organization's members weren't trained archaeologists, they conducted some investigatory digs in the area. In the 1940s and 1950s, the National Park Service began formal archaeological excavations on the foundations of other buildings at Jamestown and located a cemetery. Over the following decades, many more foundations and thousands of artifacts were uncovered. But no one found the remains of James Fort.

IN 1994 archaeologist William Kelso (*above*) and his team broke ground on the excavations of the Jamestown Rediscovery Project.

Those early scientists may not have found the fort simply because they didn't expect to and therefore weren't looking for it. Until the 1990s, almost every historian and archaeologist who studied Jamestown believed the fort's location had been at the eastern edge of the settlement, on an area of land that had been washed away by the James River many years ago. That would mean that no traces of the fort would ever be found.

The Jamestown Rediscovery Project proved that theory wrong in 1994. William Kelso, the project's chief archaeologist, had his own ideas about the location of James Fort. The members of the Rediscovery Project team studied historical documents and listened to oral traditions, stories that people pass down verbally from one generation to the next. The Jamestown oral traditions indicated that the fort had been near the brick church tower. Careful examination of the land near the tower convinced Kelso that the remains of James Fort had not been lost.

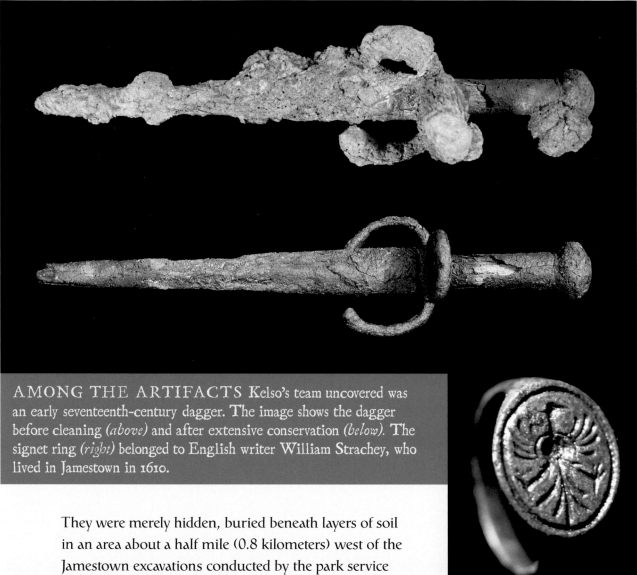

AMONG THE ARTIFACTS Kelso's team uncovered was an early seventeenth-century dagger. The image shows the dagger before cleaning (*above*) and after extensive conservation (*below*). The signet ring (*right*) belonged to English writer William Strachey, who lived in Jamestown in 1610.

They were merely hidden, buried beneath layers of soil in an area about a half mile (0.8 kilometers) west of the Jamestown excavations conducted by the park service during the 1940s and 1950s.

The rediscovery of James Fort was so complex that whole books have been written about it. In fact, any properly executed dig is far more than just a matter of grabbing a shovel and scooping up soil. For example, archaeologists must be mindful of the changes their work creates. Excavation removes soil and other evidence of the past that can never be replaced exactly as it was. Yet new discoveries often prompt scientists to rethink their conclusions about a past excavation, so they need to be able to review the site as it was before the digging took place. For this reason, archaeologists make precise records, photos, diagrams, and maps during each step of the excavation process.

The James Fort dig began with the use of an instrument called a transit to measure and establish a grid of 10-foot (3-meter) squares. This grid enabled the team to precisely identify the areas they excavated and to map the location of every discovery. Next, the archaeologists carefully removed soil from specific squares in measured levels, looking for artifacts. They also watched for changes in the soil's color or texture, which could indicate the presence of features—evidence of past occupation such as fireplaces or wells.

The team found all these things and more. Between 1994 and 1996, they uncovered tens of thousands of seventeenth-century artifacts including pottery, beads, coins, bottles, tools, armor, parts of weapons, and other military objects. Many were dated to periods before 1610, indicating that they were used during Jamestown's earliest days. The excavation also revealed features such as floors, brick fireplaces, trash pits, and wells. These finds—particularly the military objects—seemed to support the idea that the archaeologists had rediscovered James Fort. But they still needed conclusive proof.

THE ARTIFACTS FOUND IN WELLS, such as the one above, plus the surrounding soil layers, helped prove that the site that Kelso was excavating was James Fort.

Ultimately, it was not artifacts but soil features that provided that proof. The topsoil, or surface layer, at Jamestown is a rich, dark brown material. The layer beneath, called the subsoil, is a dense, beige orange clay. Every time the colonists built a structure or dug a grave, their tools penetrated the subsoil. Even centuries later, signs of their work—and the soil disturbances their diggings caused—remain as features called soil stains. Soil stains are areas colored differently than the soil surrounding them.

Through careful digging, the archaeologists exposed lines of circular stains in the soil where William Kelso suspected James Fort lay hidden. The circular stains were the only remaining traces of wooden logs that had been placed side by side, upright

WHEN THE COLONISTS BUILT the fort's palisade walls, they dug deeply in the soil to stabilize the logs, which were placed side by side vertically (*facing page, top*). The builders dug through the topsoil and into the subsoil, which was a different color. The logs left discolorations, or soil stains, in neat rows (*above*) that showed archaeologists the location and extent of the wall.

AN ARCHAEOLOGIST REMOVES CLAY from around a palisade post to leave behind a soil cast of the base of each side-by-side log.

into the ground, to form walls. This type of structure, called a palisade wall, was often built around a fort to provide defense. Moreover, the lines of soil stains joined together in a triangular shape that matched historical descriptions of the fort's walls. Here was the confirmation the archaeologists had sought: the shape and pattern of the soil stains could have been made only by the palisade walls of James Fort.

Within the fort's walls, Kelso's team found artifacts and soil features, as they expected. They also found graves—more than thirty of them.

In a sense, that discovery wasn't a surprise. According to the historical record, almost 40 percent of the settlers who came to the Chesapeake during the 1600s died within weeks or months of their arrival. Illness killed some, while others succumbed to starvation. The area's Native Americans fought to defend the land from the English newcomers, resulting in other deaths.

An unmarked cemetery that lay beneath the ruins of seventeenth-century buildings about 700 feet (213 m) outside the fort confirmed the high mortality rate. During the 1950s, archaeologists had located the outlines of seventy

TWO DOUBLE BURIALS were among the graves found by the team. Each grave contained two bodies that had been buried together.

graves in the burial ground and excavated several of them. These remains, plus graves that were subsequently excavated by Rediscovery Project team members, revealed the burials of eighty-three individuals.

Although Kelso and Owsley believe that this outer cemetery was used until the 1630s, artifacts found in some of the graves indicate that people were buried there during the earliest years of the fort. Many of these individuals were buried quickly, as if the colonists had been in a rush. This evidence suggests that these burials contain the remains of colonists who died during the winter of 1609–1610. The historical record reveals that so many colonists perished from disease and lack of food during this period that it became known as the Starving Time. In fact, Kelso estimates that more than 150 of Jamestown's 215 colonists lost their lives that winter. The deaths occurred so frequently that at times the survivors buried two and even three bodies in the same grave.

Why did the Jamestown colonists have two cemeteries, one inside the fort and one outside? There are several possible answers to this question. The historical record mentions that violent conflicts with Indians occurred during the summer of 1607. At times, the fort was under siege and it wasn't safe for the settlers to leave the fort to bury their dead. The colonists also didn't want the Native Americans to know how many men had died. They may have felt that revealing this weakening of their numbers would make their enemies bolder. On the other hand, if the Indians believed that the settlers still had a strong force, perhaps they would be less likely to attack.

The archaeologists are also considering a different theory. Most of the graves inside the fort are grouped near the southwestern end of the fort, around an open area that contains no graves. Archaeologist Carter C. Hudgins thinks the team has figured out why. "The graves may be clustered around a church," he explained. Cemeteries are commonly located alongside churches, and the historical record does mention that a church was built inside the fort. As long as burial space was still available inside the fort, the colonists may have preferred to bury their dead alongside the church. "We still need to find the remains of the church to support this theory," Hudgins added.

Since graves are often found in unexpected places, how do archaeologists first know that they may have located one—especially if it is unmarked and covered with soil that no one has dug up for centuries? Once again, the most important clues are often in the soil itself.

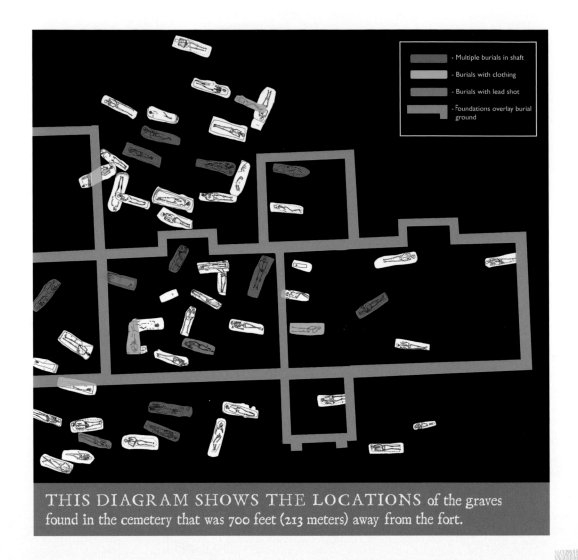

THIS DIAGRAM SHOWS THE LOCATIONS of the graves found in the cemetery that was 700 feet (213 meters) away from the fort.

Under the Soil

While it's easy to locate graves in a cemetery with headstones, unless a person has been trained in archaeology, an unmarked grave may not be immediately obvious. Most burials are first noticed as stains on the surface of the subsoil. When people bury a body, they dig a pit called a grave shaft. After placing the body in the grave, they backfill (fill in) the shaft with the soil that had been removed. Because the backfill soil contains the mixed soils of the excavated layers, it is a different color than the soil that forms the walls of the grave shaft. The result is a stain that remains even centuries later. When archaeologists uncover a soil stain that approaches 6 feet (2 m) long by 2 feet (0.6 m) wide—about the length and width of an adult human body or its coffin—they become fairly confident they've found a grave.

western palisade wall

THE RECTANGULAR DARK SOIL STAINS indicate grave shafts. The grave shaft parallel to the western palisade wall contained the remains that were later labeled JR1225B.

Such a stain was the first sign of the grave that contained the teenage boy whose bones were later examined by Doug Owsley. As the archaeologists scraped the subsoil surface, their trowels exposed a dark area. They scraped the soil further until they had exposed the complete stain. It was sized and shaped perfectly for a human grave.

At this point, the team shifted to a standard procedure for grave excavations. "[First,] we . . . take a photo of the stain of [the] grave shaft," explained William Kelso. The photograph serves as a permanent record of the appearance of the stain prior to excavation. Next, soil is removed and placed in buckets. As each bucket is taken out of the grave shaft, its contents are sifted through a mesh screen with holes measuring 0.25 inches (6.4 millimeters) on each side. As Kelso noted, "We screen every bit of grave shaft soil" to ensure that not even the tiniest artifact is overlooked.

Some artifacts—buttons and coins, for example—can be dated, which helps to establish a time frame for the burial.

In the Chesapeake area, most seventeenth-century colonial skeletons are buried at a depth of 2.5 to 4.0 feet (0.8 to 1.2 m). "We never know exactly how deeply buried the individual is going to be," explained Hudgins, "so we have to use caution." As the archaeologist reaches the depth where remains are first likely to be encountered, the pace of work slows.

The archaeologists keep their eyes peeled for all signs of burial, not just bones. They look for surviving remnants of coffins, such as bits of wood or nails. Such objects may provide useful information when they're analyzed in the laboratory. In the case of the teenage boy's grave, however, the archaeologists found no evidence of a coffin.

As the excavation of the shaft progressed, the team's anticipation grew. No matter how high the level of excitement may be at an archaeological dig, nothing can be permitted to disrupt the meticulous use of scientific methods and procedures. Proper excavation requires that every feature and found object be given a unique identifying number. The grave Hudgins was excavating was designated JR1225. The initials stand for Jamestown Rediscovery, while the number represents the complete grave as a specific feature. Unique features and objects found within the grave would be assigned a letter, in order of discovery. The first of these, the soil that filled the grave shaft, was JR1225A.

Hudgins dug further until a flash of tan caught his eye. As he wiped away the soil, he saw bone. The Jamestown Rediscovery Project was about to meet JR1225B.

Chapter Two

WHO WERE YOU?

To hear Carter Hudgins talk about finding bones is to understand what makes moments like the unearthing of JR1225B so extraordinary. "As an archaeologist, I study the material remains of the past in order to understand the histories and cultures of the past," he observed. "Most of the time, archaeology concerns the recovery and analysis of artifacts. But in the case of discovering a grave, I actually come face to face with the people I am studying. This, to me, is fascinating and moving; you actually are meeting the people of the past. They, of course, cannot talk, but they can inform us of the past through proper analysis."

With the confirmation that the shaft did indeed contain human remains, the archaeologists turned to the careful and responsible excavation of their find. It was a task that would take Hudgins and team member Danny Schmidt several days and call on their specialized knowledge of human decomposition.

As happens when any organism dies, the remains of a dead human being gradually decay. While a person is alive, muscles and bands of strong tissue called ligaments hold the bones in place. After death, microbes such as bacteria feed on these tissues along with the other parts of the body, causing them to decay.

While this process may sound revolting to us, it's actually a fundamental

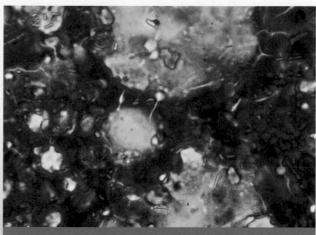

THIS MAGNIFICATION shows the type of bacteria that typically helps a dead body's tissues to decay. This natural cycle leaves behind just the bones.

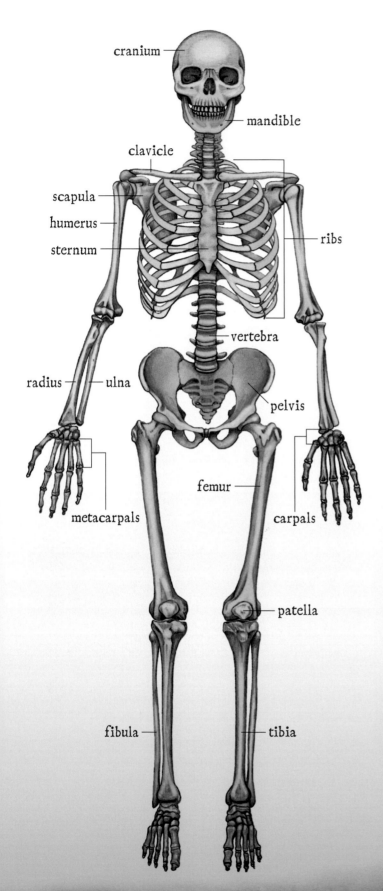

cranium

mandible

clavicle

scapula

humerus

sternum

ribs

vertebra

radius — ulna

pelvis

metacarpals

femur

carpals

patella

fibula — tibia

step in the cycle of life. As microbes consume dead tissues to extract nutrients, the tissues are broken apart on a chemical level. They decompose into the elements they're composed of, such as carbon and nitrogen. These elements are recycled when they pass out of a microbe's system and into the soil, where they provide nutrients for other animals and plants.

The tissue-dissolving action of microbes is one reason why bones are often the only remains found in graves. It also explains why those bones aren't found as close together or in as orderly a pattern as an untrained person might expect. Hudgins knew that the first step was to locate the boy's cranium, the part of the skull that encloses the brain. "It's typically the highest point of the skeletal remains," Hudgins explained, "because the rib cage collapses and other bones settle" as the soft tissues that surround them decompose.

Typically, rib bones collapse into the chest area and settle near or on top of the vertebrae, the bones that make up a person's backbone. Because most bones settle in this manner, the skull is often a little bit closer to the surface than the rest of the skeleton. "For this reason, we generally uncover the cranium completely and then progress down the body," Hudgins explained.

The sharp point and edge of a metal trowel can easily nick a bone or even flake pieces from its surface. Before continuing the excavation, Hudgins and Schmidt switched from metal trowels to wood and plastic tools, which are softer than metal and less likely to cause damage. With these tools, they uncovered the top portion of the entire skeleton.

Hudgins and Schmidt weren't surprised to find that the teenager's skeleton was quite fragile, even for bones four centuries old. This fragility is characteristic of many Jamestown skeletons, thanks to the same beige orange, clay-filled subsoil that created the telltale posthole soil stains proving the team had found James Fort. Clay holds moisture longer than many other types of soil. Year after year, each time it rained on the boy's grave, water trickled down through the soil that filled the grave shaft. The rainwater drained away slowly from the dense, clay-filled subsoil. In the meantime, the boy's bones absorbed some of this moisture, causing them to expand slightly. After the water drained away, the bones dried, which made them contract. This alternating cycle of expansion and contraction caused tiny flecks of bone to break off. On a scale of one to ten, with ten being a skeleton in perfect condition, Hudgins estimated the condition of the boy's skeleton at only a three or four.

DANNY SCHMIDT *(left)* and **C**arter Hudgins *(right)* are removing soil from around JR1225B's bones to fully expose the skeleton—a technique called pedastaling.

Up on a Pedestal

In theory, the team could have continued the excavation and started to remove the bones from the grave for further study. But once a skeleton has been moved, it isn't possible to re-create the burial scene with complete accuracy, especially if the bones are in poor condition. A forensic anthropologist such as Doug Owsley can gather many significant pieces of evidence by examining the bone in situ. (*In situ* is a Latin term meaning "in the exact position and place where an object is first found.") For this reason, the team's focus was not on removing the bones quickly but rather on preparing them for evaluation by Owsley.

As Hudgins explained, "The next step was to pedestal the bones. In this process we remove all the soil surrounding the bones except for that which is directly under them.... The bones are left lying on a pad of soil." Pedestaling results in the highest possible visibility of the details of a skeleton as well as its position in the grave.

As Hudgins pedestaled the bones, he noticed that the bones of the legs and feet were arranged in a straight line. That is, the legs were positioned close together at the knees, ankles, and feet, with the toes pointed straight up in the air. These were signs that the boy's body had been shrouded, or wrapped in a cloth, before it was buried. Because fabric decays more slowly than organic tissues, the shroud would have held the boy's bones close together even after his muscles and ligaments had decomposed. If a shroud had not been present to hold the bones in place, several inches of space would have eventually separated the boy's left and right legs and the feet would have splayed, with the toes pointing outward.

BECAUSE JR1225B'S LEG BONES were so close together, Hudgins and Kelso concluded the remains had been shrouded.

The practice of shrouding was a customary manner of caring for the dead. Seventeenth-century Chesapeake colonists were not usually buried wearing their clothes. Instead, the person who had died was wrapped from head to toe in a shroud. The shroud was held in place with ropes tied above the head and below the feet or with pins.

Archaeologists have noted a few exceptions to this custom. Some graves, including a few in the Starving Time cemetery outside James Fort, include buttons and other evidence of clothing. William Kelso and Doug Owsley feel certain that these individuals were buried in fear and haste. For the settlers, the fear of catching a contagious disease by handling the clothes of an infected person would have far outweighed the benefits of touching the body to shroud it.

The signs of shrouding that Hudgins observed as he pedestaled JR1225B's bones indicated that his remains had been treated with care, according to custom. Yet Hudgins saw other signs that seemed to indicate that the body may not have been shrouded. The boy's arms weren't at his sides or in any other dignified position consistent with a seventeenth-century shrouded English burial. His left arm lay across his body. His right arm was flung outward and upward, toward his

CLOSE STUDY OF THE POSITION of JR1225B's arms led to a discussion of seventeenth-century burial techniques. After death many early colonists were disrobed, cleaned, and wrapped in a long, narrow piece of cloth called a shroud. Shrouding typically kept the limbs from moving around. Kelso's team concluded JR1225B had been shrouded, but the shroud had been loose at the upper body.

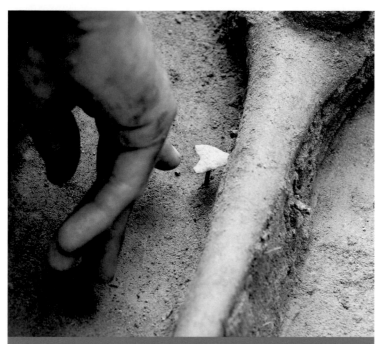

THE ARROWHEAD lying near JR1225B's left femur raised questions as to how severely the person had been wounded.

shoulder. Did this strange position indicate that no shroud had been used to hold his limbs in place?

Hudgins and Kelso didn't think so. Often a shroud was wrapped loosely around the deceased person's chest before it was tied shut above the head. If the boy had been shrouded in that fashion, there would have been room for his arms to shift, perhaps as his body was lowered into the grave. Despite the arms being askew, the close proximity of JR1225B's legs and feet, along with the position of the toes, provided sufficient evidence to confirm the presence of a shroud.

Hudgins made another, less common discovery as he continued to pedestal JR1225B's bones. Alongside the left femur—the upper leg bone—lay a white triangular arrowhead, its point almost touching the bone. The arrowhead was the type of projectile point made and used by the Powhatan Indians, who lived in the area at that time. Its presence was "a very clear indication that he was wounded," stated Hudgins. Had the wound been a factor in the boy's death?

Perhaps Doug Owsley could shed some light on that question. But before he tried to interpret the meaning of the arrowhead, he would have many other puzzles to consider.

How Old Were You?

A person's age at the time of death is one of the first things forensic anthropologists try to determine when they examine remains. When Owsley knelt on the soil next to JR1225B's grave, he began his investigation by considering the length of the long bones of the skeleton's arms and legs. Long bones grow from a person's birth until the body becomes fully mature, around the time of young adulthood. For example, the femurs of the same person compared at ages two and twelve are likely to have almost doubled in length. In the case of JR1225B, the length of the long bones quickly told Owsley that the skeleton was not that of a very young child.

To obtain a more precise age estimate, he had to look closer. Long bones have two main parts: the shaft (the long, straight part of the bone) and the epiphyses (the bony caps located at the ends of long bones). Epiphyses remain separate from the shaft during an individual's growth years. In skeletal studies, they provide an important clue to the age at death. Until the age of about fourteen, a living person's epiphyses are joined to the shaft by cartilage, the same flexible connective tissue found in the tip of the nose.

Over the course of the teen years, the epiphyses and shafts of the various long bones start to fuse together and the cartilage between them is gradually replaced by bone. At this stage, a visible line remains at the places where the epiphyses and the shafts connect. When a female reaches the ages of fourteen to eighteen, the epiphyses begin to fuse solidly to the shafts. The line where the bones have fused together disappears as the teen ages further. The epiphyses of a male's long bones fuse two to three years later than

TO DETERMINE JR1225B'S AGE, Doug Owsley examined the upper leg bone. The bone on the left belongs to JR1225B. The bony caps at the ends of the bone were not fused to the long part, indicating that JR1225B was still a teenager. The leg bone on the right belongs to a fully mature person. All parts of the bone have completely fused together.

those of a female. (This fact would come into play when Owsley later considered whether the bones were those of a male or a female.) Inspection of the skeleton's long bones revealed that the epiphyses were still unfused, a definite sign the individual was a teenager at the time of death.

Teeth also provide important clues about a person's age at death because they appear at fairly predictable times in all humans. A newborn infant usually has no visible teeth, but they are beginning to form in the jaw, below the surface of the gum. By the age of two, the child has about twenty visible teeth—often called baby teeth.

Children lose their first baby teeth when they are five to six years old. At this age, they get their first set of molars, the large, flat teeth at the back of the mouth.

HUMAN TOOTH DEVELOPMENT *by* AGE

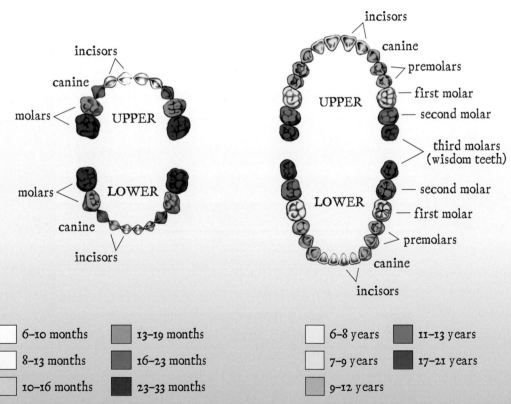

TYPICAL CHILD (*2 years old*)

incisors
canine
molars
UPPER

molars
LOWER
canine
incisors

TYPICAL ADULT (*25 years old*)

incisors
canine
premolars
first molar
second molar
UPPER

third molars
(wisdom teeth)

second molar
first molar
LOWER
premolars
canine
incisors

	6–10 months		13–19 months
	8–13 months		16–23 months
	10–16 months		23–33 months

	6–8 years		11–13 years
	7–9 years		17–21 years
	9–12 years		

The second set of molars grows in at about twelve years of age. A person's third and last set of molars, often called wisdom teeth, grows in at about eighteen years of age. The presence or absence of these various kinds of teeth helps a forensic anthropologist estimate the person's age.

JR1225B's teeth supplied additional support for Owsley's theory about the boy's age at death. The second set of molars had grown in, and the cusps— the ridged points on a tooth's surface— showed signs of wear. During colonial times, the corn and wheat used in everyday meal preparation were not ground as finely as they are in modern factories, so those people commonly ate larger pieces of grain than modern people do. Because this grittier grain was harder on the teeth, it noticeably wore them down. This type of wear is not seen on teeth in modern times. The wear on JR1225B's molars indicated that they had been used for a few years. The wisdom teeth, however, were still inside their jaw sockets, a sign that the teen was younger than eighteen or nineteen years old.

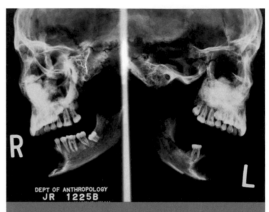

DEPT OF ANTHROPOLOGY
JR 1225B

TO FURTHER DETERMINE JR1225B's age, Owsley also looked at the teeth by X-raying the jaw. Owsley found that the wisdom teeth had not yet come in but that the second molars were worn down. This evidence placed JR1225B's age at the mid-teens.

He or She?

After determining the age of a skeleton at the time of death, the next question the forensic anthropologist tries to answer is whether the person was male or female. In the case of early Jamestown, the historical record tells us that all English colonists who arrived in 1607 were male. But a number of women arrived the following year. Since JR1225B could have been buried at any point within the twenty years James Fort was used, the remains could have been either sex.

In adult-sized skeletons, an individual's sex is determined based on variations in the pelvis. An adult female's pelvis is shaped differently from a male's, allowing room for an infant to pass between a mother's pelvic bones during childbirth.

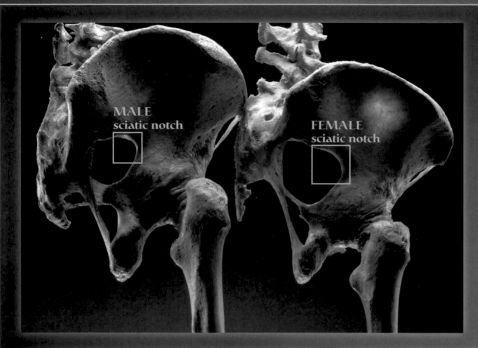

DIFFERENCES IN THE SHAPES of certain bones help forensic anthropologists determine gender. A notch called a sciatic notch is wider in a female's pelvic bones *(left)*. Certain areas of the male skull are more prominent than corresponding areas on a female's skull *(below left)*. A male's long bones, such as the upper arm bone, are usually larger and more robust than a female's *(below right)*. These kinds of differences enabled Owsley to determine that JR1225B was a male.

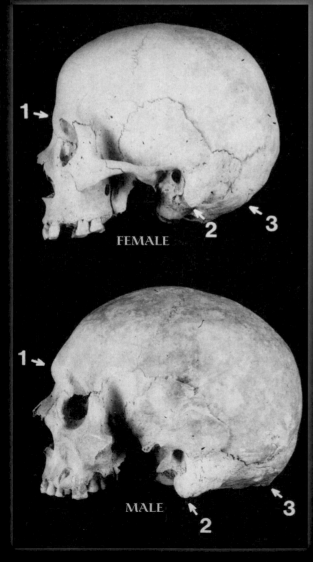

Also, the hip bones, which are part of the pelvis, are shaped differently in women than in men. Although JR1225B wasn't an adult, the features of the skeleton's pelvis were distinctly male.

Other skeletal evidence provided further support for this theory. A male's long bones are usually larger and more robust than a female's of a similar age. Men often have larger teeth than women too. JR1225B's remains met these criteria.

Perhaps most conclusive were features Owsley found on the skull. The back of a male's skull, where a muscle is attached during life, has a larger ridge than a female's skull. Males also have a more prominent brow ridge—the bony part of the skull above the eyes—than females. The chin tends to be more squared in males, while a female's chin is rounded, with the center of the chin tending to come to a point. The ridge at the back of the Jamestown teen's skull, a slightly heavier brow ridge, and a squared chin were characteristic of a male skull. This evidence, along with that of the other bones, made Owsley feel confident in asserting that JR1225B was male.

Where Did You Come From?

Another step in unraveling the mystery of a set of human remains is to try to determine the individual's ancestry. All organisms—including humans—adapt to their environment in ways that make their survival easier. Parents pass along these adaptations, including physical traits and characteristics such as skin color or hair texture, to their offspring. While each person is unique, over many generations, some traits may start to occur in recognizable patterns.

In the modern world, people from many geographical areas travel far and wide, building new cultures and starting families, sometimes with people whose ancestry differs from their own. In the colonial Chesapeake region, though, people came from three distinct ancestries: African, European, and Native American.

Certain features of a person's skull can provide clues about which population a skeleton may have belonged to. This information can be critically important in helping us understand how people lived in the past. That said, forensic anthropologists always keep in mind that each person is an individual. A given population may include many variations in bone features, and circumstances such as diet and disease may also affect the appearance of bones. Thus it's important not to rush to conclusions about any individual's ancestry.

COMPARING SKULL FEATURES of
THREE DISTINCT CHESAPEAKE GROUPS

AFRICAN

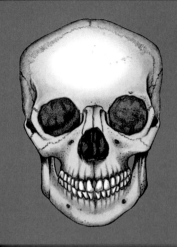

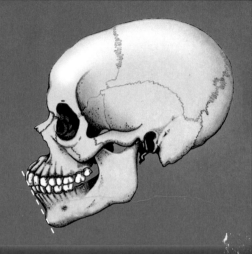

- rounded forehead

- wide nasal opening

- slight overbite

- front of jaw forward
  of chin

EUROPEAN

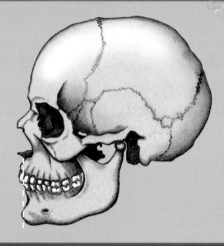

- narrow face

- narrow nasal opening

- slight overbite

- front of jaw aligned
  with chin

NATIVE AMERICAN

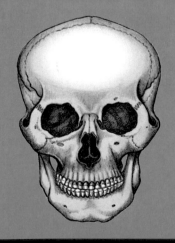

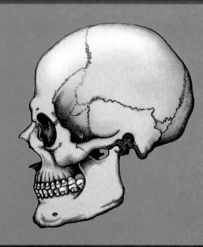

- flat face

- no overbite

- cheekbones project
  farther forward

SCHMIDT (*left*) AND HUDGINS measured JR1225B's remains in situ.

When Owsley began his study of JR1225B's skull, he looked for specific characteristics in the nose, cheeks, and jaw. For example, many, though not all, people from Africa and their descendants tend to have a wide nasal opening and a rounded forehead. The front of the jaw often protrudes farther forward than the chin. Europeans and their descendants usually have a narrow nasal opening and a narrow face. The front of the jaw is usually in line with the chin. Native Americans and their descendants generally have a flatter face than either of the other two groups, with cheekbones that project farther forward.

The front teeth of Africans and Europeans usually close together with an overbite, meaning that the upper teeth are slightly in front of the lower teeth. People of Native American ancestry don't tend to have an overbite. When the mouth is closed, the upper and lower front teeth usually meet edge to edge. Even slight differences in the shape of the bones that form the roof of the mouth can help identify whether colonial-period remains are African, European, or Native American.

Ultimately, it's a combination of observation, laboratory testing, and precise measurement that enables forensic anthropologists to decide upon the most likely ancestry of a particular set of remains. Even without all of these tools, however, Owsley could see that JR1225B's skull features—the narrow nasal opening, the narrow face, and the shape of the bones of the roof of his mouth—were like those of English people of the seventeenth century. Using these criteria, Owsley determined that the teenager buried inside James Fort was European.

Owsley concluded his initial examination of JR1225B by asking Hudgins and Schmidt to measure the full skeleton and the long bones of the legs. "We measure bones in situ for many reasons. At Jamestown, I've got to measure in place or I'm not going to get the measurement of the whole bone," Owsley explained. Poorly preserved bones—which are common at Jamestown due to the clay subsoil—often crumble as they are removed from the grave. The fragments may be reassembled in the laboratory, but they won't exactly replicate their appearance and size in the grave.

Next, Owsley took a close look at the arrowhead Hudgins had spotted. It could have remained so close to the boy's femur throughout decomposition only if it had been deeply embedded in his thigh muscle. Although many more colonists died from starvation and disease, some colonists died from wounds received in skirmishes with Native Americans. Had the boy died as a result of such a wound?

Owsley's opinion was that the boy wouldn't have died immediately of the wound. It was in a fleshy area of the leg where a major blood vessel wasn't likely to have been severed. However, infection was common in the colonial Chesapeake region due to lack of medical knowledge about cleanliness and the care of wounds. If the boy's wound had become infected, harmful bacteria would have quickly spread throughout his body, resulting in blood poisoning. A fast-acting infection of this sort can kill a person in a matter of days and does not leave traces in the bones. Further analysis of the boy's bones in Owsley's laboratory would supply information about the boy's life and death, though whether it would solve this particular puzzle remained to be seen.

Chapter Three

OUT OF THE GRAVE

JR1225B's BONES WERE SO FRAGILE that they had to be removed from his grave with the supporting soil of the pedestal still beneath them. Otherwise, they would have crumbled to bits. With the soil still in place, the bones were carefully transferred onto trays and sent for conservation, a treatment process to protect them from decay and damage. Although archaeologists may begin this process while the bones are in situ, Kelso's team felt that conserving JR1225B's bones in the lab would be easier.

This process took place at the Jamestown Rediscovery Project's conservation laboratory near the excavation site. First, senior conservator Michael Lavin set aside several untreated bone samples to send to Owsley for scientific analyses that require bone material that has not been conserved.

Using soft brushes, dental picks, and specially treated water, Lavin removed all traces of the soil that clung to JR1225B's bones. The next

A CLOSE-UP of JR1225B's skull shows how fragile the bones were.

step, drying the skeleton, took a remarkable two weeks. "Although the skeletal material may appear dry [within hours], it still retains some moisture," Lavin stated. This hidden moisture must be removed gradually to prevent the bones from shrinking, much as they had in the grave after heavy rains. Lavin further explained that conservation experts solve this problem "by placing the bones in drying racks and covering them with plastic perforated with small holes." The holes control the amount of air that reaches the bones, slowing the drying process.

Next, Lavin coated the bones with an acrylic mixture that acts like glue, binding the bone tightly to prevent breakage or flaking. After the mixture dried, he fitted together fragments of broken bones and glued them as well. Finally, he wrapped JR1225B's labeled, conserved bones with a clear, plastic material specially made for protecting fragile items and placed them in storage boxes. To prevent damage from changes in the atmosphere, the boxes were kept in a temperature-controlled and humidity-controlled vault until they were sent to Owsley's forensic laboratory at the Smithsonian Institution.

CAREFUL CONSERVATION TECHNIQUES are used to protect skeletal remains from further damage. Lavin applies an acrylic mixture to bones in situ. For JR1225B, this process was done in the lab.

There, Owsley and his colleague Kari Bruwelheide, a skeletal biologist and forensic anthropologist, laid the skeleton on a table, each bone in its anatomically correct position. Using a magnifying lens, they examined each bone and tooth and made notes of their observations. Next, Owsley and Bruwelheide used precise measuring tools called calipers to measure JR1225B's long bones. (These measurements are compared with those that were made in situ to confirm their accuracy.) By plugging these measurements into a mathematical formula, they determined the teenager's height was about 5 feet 8 inches (1.7 m)—unusually tall for the seventeenth century. And he was still growing! After the measurements were taken, the forensic anthropologists set aside additional bone and tooth samples for laboratory tests.

The scientists turned their attention to the femur next to which the arrowhead had been found. Close examination confirmed Owsley's initial opinion at the gravesite: the arrowhead had not penetrated or damaged the femur in any visible way. That still left the possibility the wound had become infected and had led to blood poisoning, which would have killed the boy without causing any damage to the bone.

Forensic examination of a different bone—the boy's right clavicle, or collarbone—provided another clue. The clavicle had been fractured. Its broken edges hadn't healed at all, indicating that the break must have occurred shortly before the boy died. (This injury helps explain why the boy's right arm and shoulder had slid into such an awkward, abnormal position as he was placed in his grave. The shoulder could slide into that position only because the clavicle was broken.) Together, the arrow wound and the broken clavicle led Owsley and Bruwelheide to conclude that the boy had likely died as a result of violence.

WHEN JR1225B'S BODY WAS PLACED in the grave, his broken clavicle shifted into an abnormal position beneath the skull. That caused his arm to slide into a position that would have been otherwise impossible.

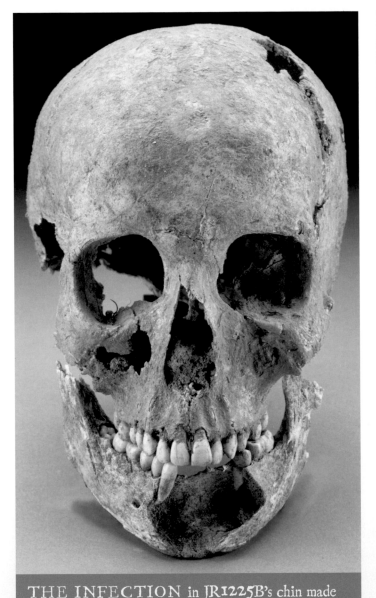

THE INFECTION in JR1225B's chin made the bone so brittle that parts of it crumbled away after burial.

TWO OF THE TEETH in the lower part of the jaw had been broken. The exposed pulp inside one of them opened the door to infection.

The boy had other health issues too. A depression in the front of his skull, above his left eye socket, revealed that he had sustained a blow to the head that had healed before his death. The bone in the roofs of his eye sockets contained small holes, a sign that his diet lacked sufficient iron. And X-rays of the boy's leg bones showed bands called Harris lines, which form when the growth of a bone repeatedly stops and restarts. Such disruptions of growth are a result of poor nutrition or the stress of disease.

The most serious problem by far, however, was a raging, ongoing infection in the boy's lower jaw, where two central incisors were damaged. The left incisor was broken in half, exposing the pulp, the soft inner part of a tooth that contains the nerves and blood vessels. At first, the injury would have caused intense pain, particularly at mealtimes, because the exposed pulp chamber would have been extremely sensitive to cold and heat. The boy probably covered the broken tooth with his lower lip and tongue to protect the exposed nerve from hot and cold foods. Within ten days, as the pulp deteriorated, a pus-filled area called an abscess formed at the tooth's root. After a week or two, the nerve of the tooth died, ending the pain the boy felt from hot and cold substances.

The problem hadn't gone away, though. Owsley saw signs that the abscess spread, further inflaming the bone socket and the surrounding gum tissue. During a period of several months, bacteria and infection spread into the bone of the boy's chin and jaw. Once the infection had spread that far, JR1225B would have been in severe pain again—possibly worse than before. Left unchecked, the infection would have affected his immune system. Colonial people often died from infections that modern antibiotic medicines can cure. Depending on the type of bacteria involved, the severity of JR1225B's infection would have soon caused him to die. It's likely that the boy's sudden death as a result of the arrowhead wound only shortened his life by a few months, if not weeks.

If the Jamestown teenager were alive today, his broken tooth could have been treated. An endodontist—a dentist who specializes in diseases of the tooth pulp—would drill the nerve out of the broken tooth's root and pack the empty root canal with a filling material. Modern painkillers make this procedure far less excruciating than the suffering JR1225B endured. Finally, a dentist would replace the top part of the broken tooth with a false crown made of a tooth-colored, porcelainlike material. Within days, the boy would have been enjoying his meals without any problem.

He Ate Like an Englishman

One kind of laboratory test critical to forensic anthropology is called stable isotope analysis. Stable isotope analyses can supply information about a person's diet and, in the case of some colonial settlers, provide clues to the settler's birthplace and how long he or she had lived in America. The stories gleaned from laboratory examinations and tests are detailed, fascinating, and sometimes shocking.

The next facts that JR1225B's bones revealed came via a chemical element called carbon. When green plants undergo the nutrient-making process of photosynthesis, they absorb varying amounts of three forms, or isotopes, of this element: carbon-12, carbon-13, and carbon-14. Carbon-12 has six protons and six neutrons in the nucleus of each atom. Carbon-13 has six protons and seven neutrons, and carbon-14 contains six protons and eight neutrons. Carbon-12 and carbon-13 are called stable isotopes because they do not break down over time, as carbon-14 does.

All three isotopes are absorbed by bones when people consume green plants. Carbon-13 is of particular interest to forensic anthropologists for two reasons. First, the amount of carbon-13 that bones absorb varies depending on the type of plants a person eats. Second, as a stable isotope, carbon-13 remains in a person's bones after death and can be measured even centuries later. These two characteristics enable scientists to determine what plants the person ate and sometimes—based on where those plants commonly grow—where the person lived.

carbon-12
stable

carbon-13
stable

carbon-14
unstable (radioactive)

In colonial Chesapeake studies, the key plant is corn, which grows in many parts of North America and contains more carbon-13 than many other grains. Corn played a significant part in the diets of Native Americans and colonists. Before their arrival in North America, however, the colonists would have eaten grains that were commonly grown in Europe—barley, wheat, and rye, for example—which contain a much lower amount of carbon-13.

As a person's diet changes, the nutrients that the body transports to the bones reflect the new foods. Over time, the bones themselves change. For example, when people born in England moved to the American colonies and started to eat more corn, the level of carbon-13 in their bones slowly increased. Scientists think that it takes about twenty years for a bone's carbon-13 content to be completely replaced by dietary change.

The amount of carbon-13 found in bones can be measured and analyzed based on scientific research to determine a number known as the carbon-13 value. This value is written as a negative number—that is, a number less than zero. A person born and raised in England, for example, typically has a carbon-13 level with a value between –21 and –18. The carbon-13 value for a person born and raised in North America on a diet that included corn would be in the range of –15 to –9. Scientists believe that a value between –18 and –16 in a colonial American's remains indicates that the colonist was probably born and raised in England and immigrated to North America, where he or she lived less than twenty years before death.

The isotope analysis of the samples taken from JR1225B's bones revealed a carbon-13 value of –19.3. "The value of –19.3 is very English, with absolutely no corn influencing his diet," Bruwelheide noted. Because the amount of carbon-13 in the boy's bones is so low, Owsley and Bruwelheide are confident that he had only recently arrived from England when he died. "The isotope analysis fits perfectly with JR1225B's identity as a boy likely in service to one or more of the men, or a ship's boy who was killed shortly after arriving in Virginia," Bruwelheide added. In fact, he may have been a victim of a documented Indian attack on James Fort that took place on May 25, 1607. One colonial document, which describes this attack, mentions that a boy was killed.

The historical evidence uncovered so far supports this theory. Catherine Correll Walls volunteers as an historian for the Association for the Preservation of Virginia Antiquities. One of her goals is to identify JR1225B by researching the historical record. At least four boys were known to have been on the three ships that arrived in Jamestown in 1607 and were therefore likely candidates. Reading journals, church records, and many other materials, Correll Walls meticulously traced leads for each name. Two of the boys are mentioned as being alive in journal accounts in 1608, so they clearly hadn't died in 1607. According to records found in England, the third boy would have been nine years old that year, too young to be JR1225B.

The last and, Correll Walls believes, most likely candidate is a young man named Richard Mutton.

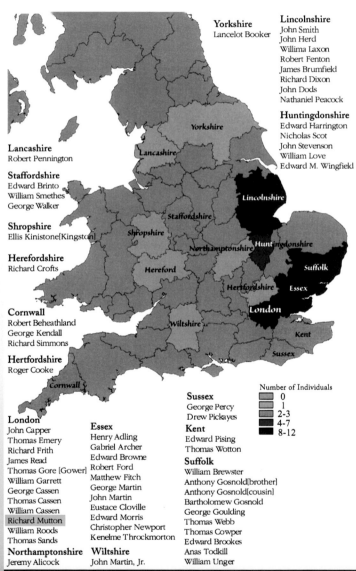

Yorkshire
Lancelot Booker

Lincolnshire
John Smith
John Herd
Willima Laxon
Robert Fenton
James Brumfield
Richard Dixon
John Dods
Nathaniel Peacock

Huntingdonshire
Edward Harrington
Nicholas Scot
John Stevenson
William Love
Edward M. Wingfield

Lancashire
Robert Pennington

Staffordshire
Edward Brinto
William Smethes
George Walker

Shropshire
Ellis Kinistone[Kingston]

Herefordshire
Richard Crofts

Cornwall
Robert Beheathland
George Kendall
Richard Simmons

Hertfordshire
Roger Cooke

London
John Capper
Thomas Emery
Richard Frith
James Read
Thomas Gore [Gower]
William Garrett
George Cassen
Thomas Cassen
William Cassen
Richard Mutton
William Roods
Thomas Sands

Northamptonshire
Jeremy Alicock

Essex
Henry Adling
Gabriel Archer
Edward Browne
Robert Ford
Matthew Fitch
George Martin
John Martin
Eustace Cloville
Edward Morris
Christopher Newport
Kenelme Throckmorton

Wiltshire
John Martin, Jr.

Sussex
George Percy
Drew Pickayes

Kent
Edward Pising
Thomas Wotton

Suffolk
William Brewster
Anthony Gosnold[brother]
Anthony Gosnold[cousin]
Bartholomew Gosnold
George Goulding
Thomas Webb
Thomas Cowper
Edward Brookes
Anas Todkill
William Unger

Number of Individuals
0
1
2-3
4-7
8-12

A MAP OF SOUTHERN ENGLAND shows the places of origin of some of the first Jamestown colonists. Richard Mutton's name is toward the end of the left column.

"Richard Mutton is listed by John Smith as one of the boys that arrived in Virginia in May of 1607. His name does not appear again in [the] records," she explained. "We have not determined the exact birthplace or birth date for Richard, but I have located one possibility in a [baptism] record for 2nd June, 1593, [in] London, England."

Richard Mutton certainly seems a fitting candidate for JR1225B. His disappearance from the historical record suggests he may have died in 1607. If Correll Walls has correctly located his birth record, he was fourteen years old at the time of his death—well within Doug Owsley's age estimate for JR1225B. Still, as tantalizing as the possibility seems, JR1225B may not be Richard Mutton. Many colonists who traveled to Jamestown were not listed in the historical record, so the skeleton could belong to an unnamed boy. Only further research will determine whether the identification can be confirmed.

Chapter Four

THE CAPTAIN

THE TEENAGE BOY WHO MAY HAVE BEEN RICHARD MUTTON is one among many fascinating life stories that archaeologists and forensic anthropologists have rescued from the buried past of the colonial Chesapeake area. A different grave, found in Jamestown a few years before JR1225B, posed a set of puzzles—and possible solutions—no less compelling.

The discovery began with a trash pit that William Kelso's team of archaeologists unearthed in 2002 as they excavated alongside what had been the western wall of James Fort. Within the pit, settlers had buried typical seventeenth-century colonial trash: pieces of tobacco pipes, bricks, and oyster shells. Because these artifacts dated approximately to the 1630s, the team knew that anything beneath the trash pit would have to belong to an earlier time period.

To their surprise, what they found as they continued the dig was the telltale soil stain of a grave shaft. Most graves and graveyards are treated with respect. People wouldn't customarily bury trash above a grave

ARCHAEOLOGIST TONIA DEETZ ROCK carefully brushes away soil from the skull of remains buried outside the James Fort walls.

A LONG STAFF (*right*) was buried with the remains. The iron tip was heavily encrusted with rust. The colored pole next to the staff is a measuring tool.

unless the presence of the grave had been forgotten.

Two other interesting facts stood out. Unlike other graves found during the excavation of the fort, this grave was outside the fort, not within it. And because the grave lay parallel to the fort's wall, the team knew that the wall must have already been standing at the time the shaft was dug.

As Kelso's team excavated the grave shaft, they screened the backfill soil that had been used to fill it centuries before. They found no colonial artifacts in the soil. "In the earliest graves we find nothing but prehistoric materials," Kelso explained. Historians and archaeologists use the term *prehistoric* to refer to the time before written history. The lack of colonial artifacts in the backfill didn't mean that the grave was dug before the colonists came to Jamestown, though. But because it lay parallel to the fort wall, it must have been dug after the fort was built. As Kelso described, the contents of the backfill simply meant that the grave "is from a period where there isn't enough historic material around to accidentally end up in the shaft." Together with the materials in the trash pit and the presence of the fort wall, the backfill helped the team date the grave to 1607–1608.

The shape of the burial itself indicated that the remains had been enclosed in a coffin, a rare privilege for Chesapeake colonists early in the seventeenth century. Because building a coffin required time, energy, and wood that could all be used in other ways, most individuals were buried in shrouds only. The use of a coffin suggested that this grave contained the remains of a person of some importance.

When the archaeologists excavated down to the level where the coffin lid would have been, they made another unusual discovery: a rust-colored soil stain was outside the coffin. The stain, which was near the end of the coffin that contained the upper part of the body, narrowed suddenly and continued for about 5.5 feet (1.6 m). "We didn't really know what it was," Kelso recalled. The rust in the soil suggested the presence of an object made of iron, and indeed, close examination suggested that there appeared to be some sort of artifact encased in the rust. The artifact was very fragile, so it was excavated as a block, with the surrounding soil still firmly around it. The block was taken to a laboratory to be X-rayed to attempt to identify the artifact's shape before the soil was removed.

The X-ray revealed an object that the archaeologists had seen in drawings from the seventeenth century: the iron pike, or point, of a captain's leading staff, a lancelike weapon used by persons of high rank in the military. The pike fit on a long wooden pole called a shaft. In the grave, the long, thin soil stain that extended away from the rust-encrusted iron pike was the only remaining evidence of the staff's wooden shaft.

While the leading staff could have been used in combat, it's also possible that it was carried as a ceremonial weapon. A weapon like this one would have been placed in a grave only as a sign of respect and honor for a revered person. Kelso recalled, for example, that some of the courtiers who served Queen Elizabeth I of England had placed their own leading staffs in her grave as a sign of respect.

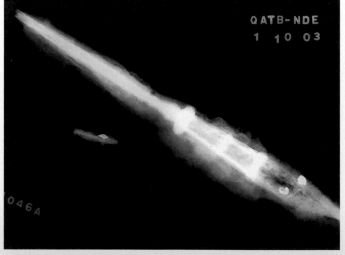

As the archaeologists continued their work, they were delighted to discover that the skeleton in the grave was very well preserved. The remains were given the official identification number of JR1046B, but the leading staff prompted the team to dub the skeleton "the Captain." Other than a few missing foot bones, the skeleton was complete. As Kelso described it, "On a scale of one to ten, the Captain is a ten." Given the poorly preserved state of other Jamestown skeletons, such as JR1225B, why were the Captain's bones in such excellent condition? After all, the Captain's bones, like the

BEFORE REMOVING THE STAFF, it was X-rayed (*top*). Then conservators cleaned it to reveal its shape (*above*).

SHROUD PINS ARE USED to hold a burial shroud in place. When they are made of copper, the pins leave behind a green stain *(above)* after they've corroded.

others in Jamestown, had undergone a destructive alternating cycle of wet and dry conditions. His wooden coffin would have quickly deteriorated, offering no long-term protection for the bones.

The answer, as in so many archaeological puzzles, is the soil. The area where the Captain was buried has sandy soil with a very different consistency than the clay-filled soil that surrounded the graves of JR1225B and other colonists buried within James Fort. Water easily drains from sand, so the soil didn't remain wet for long even after heavy rains. Because the Captain's bones hadn't lain in swampy underground puddles as the others had, they were better preserved.

This preservation helped the team readily glean useful information from the bones. For example, while JR1225B's grave and remains had required considerable analysis to determine how he was buried, Kelso immediately felt certain that "the Captain was definitely shrouded." Not only were his knees and leg bones positioned close together, but the bones from his right forearm had green stains, an unmistakable sign of decomposing shroud pins.

Shroud pins—straight pins, like those used in sewing clothes—were used to hold together parts of a shroud. Most evidence of such pins is found around the skull.

That's because when a body was shrouded, the face was often left exposed so that family members and friends could see the individual's face as they paid their last respects. Shortly before burial, a separate piece of cloth was placed over the face and pinned in place.

A SHROUD PIN from a colonial Chesapeake burial

Well-preserved shroud pins may look almost as good as new. But such preservation of colonial shroud pins, which were usually made of copper, is rare. When buried in soil over a period of centuries, copper undergoes chemical reactions that cause it to corrode, or decay. Corroded copper forms a substance called copper oxide, which leaves a green discoloration. Poorly preserved copper pins may only remain as a small green fleck or a stain on a bone or in the soil.

Doug Owsley's forensic examination of the Captain revealed more. The pelvic bones helped confirm the skeleton belonged to a male. Bony spurs called lipping had formed on the man's spine and right arm. Lipping is a sign of arthritis, a painful disease that often affects the joints of older people. The lipping on the Captain's bones was minimal, suggesting that he had just a touch of arthritis. That plus the fused epiphyses on his long bones indicated that he was between thirty-three and thirty-nine years old when he died. Features on the skull suggested he had a large, broad nose and a small, square chin. Based on the length of his leg bones, he'd been about 5 feet 3 inches (1.6 m) tall. The overall size of his bones indicated he'd been a slender rather than stocky man.

Thanks to another principle of forensic anthropology, Owsley was able to assess the Captain's level of physical activity during his lifetime. No matter how active people are, bones appear slightly thicker in the places where muscles attach to them. When a person uses the same muscles frequently over time, however, that labor is reflected by further changes in the bones. "One way a body responds to a muscle being heavily used is by building more bone mass in the area," Owsley explained. The areas where heavily used muscles are attached to bone become even more developed and defined as a result.

Owsley noted that the places where the Captain's arm muscles had been attached to the bones were slightly more developed on the right humerus—the upper arm bone—than those on the left. Still, none of the areas were as hugely developed as they would be in a person who had lived a life filled with hard labor. Observing that the lower right arm bones—the ulna and radius—were slightly longer than the left ones, Owsley concluded that the Captain had used his right arm more than the left. While never a hard laborer, he'd been a physically active, right-handed man.

During the examination of the skull, Owsley noticed that the Captain was missing a few teeth. Had the teeth fallen out after the Captain was buried—teeth often do—or before his death? In the seventeenth and eighteenth centuries, tooth loss was a common occurrence. By the time people reached their late twenties or thirties, they were likely to have already lost one tooth, if not more, as a result of decay. When Owsley took a closer look at the empty tooth sockets, he saw that new bone growth had started to fill the sockets. Bone grows only while a person is alive, so the Captain must have lost the teeth long enough before his death for new bone growth to occur. The Captain's remaining teeth showed moderate signs of wear and had a few small cavities.

As Owsley continued to examine the skull, he saw extra bone formations on the bones inside the opening where the Captain's nose had been. These kinds of changes are the result of chronic, or ongoing, infections that cause the tissues

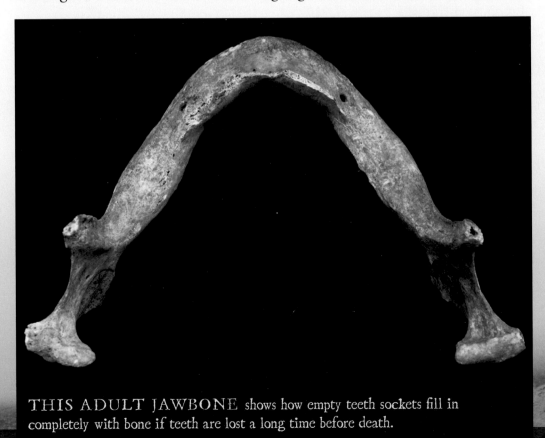

THIS ADULT JAWBONE shows how empty teeth sockets fill in completely with bone if teeth are lost a long time before death.

inside the nasal area to become inflamed. The inflammation may have made the Captain sound stuffed up, as if he had a cold, when he talked. His left ankle had small fractures—likely the result of a severely sprained ankle—that had healed before his death. Other than that, the Captain's bones showed no signs of major injury or disease.

The stable isotope analysis of the Captain's remains showed a carbon-13 value of –18.83, well in keeping with people who had been eating grains that grew in England. Owsley is certain that the Captain had not been in the Virginia colony for very long when he died. If he had, eating a steady diet filled with corn would have increased the value, making it less negative.

Putting together the forensic examination, the isotope analysis, and his knowledge of colonial social classes, Owsley concluded that the Captain had been a gentleman, a member of the educated upper class. Since no obvious signs of long-term disease or injury were present, Owsley thinks that the Captain probably died of one of the various diseases that killed colonists within days or weeks, such as dysentery. Because these kinds of sickness act so quickly, they don't leave trace evidence in the bones. Indeed, the Captain's cause of death may never be found.

The Captain's Name

The historical record supplied an intriguing clue when Kelso's team tackled their next task, that of identifying the Captain. George Percy, one of the original Jamestown colonists, kept a journal of the settlement's earliest days. A 1607 entry describes a somber yet intriguing event: "The two and twentieth day of August, there died Captain Bartholomew Gosnold, one of our council; he was honorably buried, having all the ordnance [cannons] in the fort shot off with many volleys of small shot."

From other historical records, Kelso knew that Bartholomew Gosnold was one of the captains of the three ships that reached Jamestown in 1607. He died later that summer, after an unspecified three-week illness, at the age of about thirty-five. Could this "honorably buried" man be the Captain? A leading staff like the one Kelso's team found in the Captain's grave is certainly a sign of such a burial. The use of a shroud and a coffin would have also been fitting for a man with the status of a ship's captain and a gentleman.

THE THREE SHIPS THAT SAILED up the James River in 1607 were the *Godspeed* (*left*), the *Susan Constant* (*center*), and the *Discovery* (*right*). Bartholomew Gosnold captained the *Godspeed* and died only a few months after arriving in what became Jamestown, Virginia.

Data the team had gathered via forensic analysis also fit Gosnold's biography. The Captain's age range, the evidence that he had been a gentleman rather than a hard laborer, the short span of time he'd spent in the Virginia colony, and Owsley's assessment that a brief illness had likely killed him all matched documented facts about Bartholomew Gosnold. Still, the team lacked absolute proof. The historical record revealed two other Jamestown colonists, Gabriel Archer and Ferdinando Wenman, whose age and status made them possible candidates.

Laboratory analysis of the Captain's teeth added more information to this complex puzzle. Much as a carbon-13 analysis can link a person's bones with the area where the person lived, the isotopes of two other elements—strontium and oxygen—and their levels in the teeth can do the same. Isotopes of these two elements are found in varying amounts as components of the soil in different regions. As water trickles through the soil, extremely small amounts of the isotopes are washed into it. In this way, they become part of the region's drinking water. As children drink the water, their developing teeth absorb the isotopes, which become part of the teeth's enamel, or hard outer covering. The amount of each isotope in the tooth enamel remains constant as a person grows older. By measuring these amounts and comparing them to the isotope levels in the soil of various regions, scientists can often determine where an individual grew up.

The analysis of the Captain's tooth enamel revealed that his remains may belong to Archer, who died in 1609–1610, during the Starving Time, or to Wenman, who died shortly thereafter in 1610. Both of these men grew up in parts of England with soil isotope levels consistent with those found in the Captain's tooth enamel. But the results don't rule out Gosnold. Similar soil conditions also occur not far from the place Gosnold was raised—though not in that exact location.

Kelso doesn't believe that either Archer or Wenman, although important in the Jamestown settlement, had attained a status that would have warranted placing a leading staff in their graves. That was an honor reserved for a man entitled to the highest respect, as Gosnold was. As Kelso put it, "We've got Bartholomew Gosnold . . . until it can be proven otherwise."

THE CAPTAIN'S REMAINS were put inside a coffin before being buried. Very few of the earliest Jamestown settlers warranted such honor and expense.

But why would an honored gentleman have been buried outside the fort, given that the majority of Jamestown's earliest dead—JR1225B among them—were buried within the fort, near the area where the archaeologists think a church once stood? Kelso speculated that perhaps "the Englishmen made a big ceremony out of Gosnold's burial as a show of force to quell rumors that many were dying." Burying Gosnold outside the fort, with great ceremony, might have been intended to create the appearance that this death was unusual and that the settlers were, on the whole, thriving.

Why are Kelso and his team so gratified to have identified Gosnold's remains? "He [was] very important, but we don't know much about him," explained Kelso. While the name Bartholomew Gosnold may be unfamiliar to contemporary Americans, he was well known and respected among English traders of his time. More important, he was also a driving force in the movement to bring English settlers to North America.

Five years before the Virginia Company's 1607 expedition to found Jamestown, Gosnold explored the bays along the coasts of the modern-day states of Maine and Massachusetts. In fact, he may have been the first Englishman to set foot on Massachusetts' Cape Cod, which he named in May 1602. When Gosnold returned to England, he resolved that he would see North America again. He introduced his idea to return and build a settlement to a man named John Smith. Not only did John Smith become part of the Virginia Company's expedition, he also became famously known as an early leader of Jamestown and friend of Pocahontas, daughter of the werowance (leader) of the Powhatan people.

Had Bartholomew Gosnold lived, he might have become an equally significant person in American history. Unfortunately, he died only three months after setting foot ashore at Jamestown.

For nearly a century after Gosnold's brief time in Virginia, Jamestown served as the colony's capital. During this time, English settlers founded other towns throughout the Chesapeake and other regions. In 1698, after a fire destroyed an important government building in Jamestown, the capital was moved to the city of Williamsburg. People gradually moved away from Jamestown. Over the decades, most traces of the settlement vanished, not to be rediscovered for hundreds of years.

Chapter Five

THE BODY IN THE BASEMENT

By the early 1630s, Virginia had grown into an established, profitable colony. To the northeast, several English towns had taken root in Massachusetts. In 1634 another group of eager would-be settlers arrived in the Chesapeake region from England. They founded a new colony, Maryland.

Like Jamestown's earliest settlers, the English who came to Maryland hoped to find a wealthier life in North America, but they weren't looking for gold or silver. They planned to make money by growing and selling tobacco. This crop had become wildly popular in England, where it was used for smoking and as medicine. Although tobacco couldn't grow in the cool, wet climate of England, the Chesapeake's warmer, longer growing season was perfect for it.

While the residents of Jamestown had never found the treasures they'd hoped to claim in Virginia, they did learn how to grow a type of tobacco that English buyers loved. By the time Maryland was settled in the 1630s, the plant had become almost

A HISTORICAL REENACTOR inspects tobacco plants growing in the Chesapeake area.

as valuable as gold. As archaeologist Al Luckenbach explained, "Everybody in the Chesapeake grew tobacco. That was the way you tried to get rich." In fact, as the colonists' plantations—and their profits—grew, Chesapeake settlers paid for most goods and services with tobacco instead of exchanging coins or paper money.

Given the many tobacco plantations that existed in the Maryland colony, it came as little surprise to Luckenbach that one of the most fascinating excavations of his career took place on a site that had once been a tobacco plantation. Like many extraordinary scientific discoveries, however, it began like any other research endeavor.

IN 2003 members of the Lost Towns Project began excavating Leavy Neck, the site of William Neale's small tobacco plantation in Maryland. He likely lived there from 1662 to his death in 1677.

As the director of the Lost Towns Project, Luckenbach and his team learn about colonial lives by finding and excavating long-forgotten sites in Maryland's Anne Arundel County. It was there, in 2003, that the team excavated the former home of a planter named William Neale. In colonial times, the community established in that area was called Providence. The tract of land on which Neale's plantation was located was known as Leavy Neck. For that reason, Luckenbach calls the site Leavy Neck.

According to land records from the period, Neale's plantation was about 120 acres (49 hectares), the size of almost 110 football fields. By the standard of Chesapeake farmers, it was small and "not particularly prosperous—at the time Neale would have been referred to as a middling planter," Luckenbach said.

Land ownership records indicate that Neale acquired the Leavy Neck property in 1662. Artifacts found during the excavation of the site support the team's belief that the house was built about that time. Further archaeological evidence supports the theory that the house was abandoned sometime around 1677, most likely after

A RESTORED SEVENTEENTH-CENTURY PLANTER'S HOUSE shows the storage cellar beneath the floor of the main room. (The floor planks have been removed and are stacked along the far wall.) Usually, a family stored food and other household items in this cellar. In William Neale's case, the family used it as a garbage pit.

Neale's death, which occurred that year. That meant Luckenbach's excavation of the house would reveal activity that occurred within the time period of 1662–1677.

The frame of Neale's house was fastened to posts that were sunk deeply into the soil. Like Jamestown's palisade walls, the soil stains left by the posts were the only remaining evidence of the structure. An earthen-walled cellar was located under the floorboards of the house, probably in front of the fireplace. Colonial cellars like this one were used for the storage of food, beverages in jugs, and household items. Archaeological evidence showed that Neale's cellar had also been used for another purpose—as a trash dump. "People lived upstairs and dumped fish parts and pig parts and chamber pot contents and goodness knows what else down there," explained Luckenbach. The artifacts found among the levels of trash included a coin dated 1664. Just beneath the trash and covered only by a thin layer of clay lay something much more unusual, however: a human body.

Unlike the Captain's grave in Jamestown, where a trash pit had been located on top of a long-forgotten grave, the grave in Neale's cellar was located in a building that was occupied at the time the body was buried. And at the time of the burial, the cellar floor was already littered with trash. In the years following the burial, layers of trash completely filled the cellar. The most recent artifacts in these layers date to the late 1670s. That means the burial took place before then.

The grave showed no signs of having been created with respect for the remains it contained. The shaft was poorly dug, with an uneven bottom. It wasn't even long enough. Whoever buried the person had to bend the legs to make the body fit. A large piece of broken ceramic, known to archaeologists as a sherd, lay on top of the skeleton's chest. Luckenbach recognized the sherd as part of a milk pan, a wide shallow, ceramic vessel that colonists used to hold fresh milk while cream rose to the surface. "It looked very much like the milk pan was . . . used to shove the body into the grave," Luckenbach noted. The archaeologists

IN THE PIT beneath Neale's house, archaeologists found a coin dating from 1664.

A THIN LAYER OF CLAY covered the remains of a human body, hastily dumped into the pit. Note the large piece of pottery resting on the rib cage.

found several other pieces of the milk pan among the trash nearby. It certainly appeared that the person who buried the body simply grabbed the nearest large object at hand to avoid touching the body.

Further evidence of disrespect was even more illuminating. "The body was lying on top of a broken pipe bowl, with no sign of deliberate, respectful grave goods [objects or clothing buried with a body]," Luckenbach said. Several of the bones had green stains, but they were too long and wide to be the remnants of shroud pins. The team believes the stains are remnants of an unknown metal artifact that someone had tossed into the shaft as the grave was filled. The presence and location of a bone from a cow or an ox, a nail, and two oyster shells confirmed that the cellar was definitely used as a trash pit at the time the body was placed in the grave.

A cellar dumping ground is definitely not the type of place where English colonists would have buried someone they had loved or esteemed. Luckenbach suspected that the body in Neale's cellar might have been that of a person whose loved ones, if any, were far away in England. This person must have also lacked the friends, money, or status in the Providence community to ensure a proper burial.

But why would such a person have been associated with William Neale? The answer is work. If a middling planter such as Neale hoped to raise his station in life and become more prosperous, he had to grow more tobacco. This type of farming requires a great deal of physical labor. Neale would have needed help, and he would have most likely bought–not hired–that help in the form of an indentured servant. Indeed, historical documents note that Neale, his wife, two children, and two unnamed indentured servants had lived at Leavy Neck.

During most of the seventeenth century, indentured servants were the colonial Chesapeake's main workforce. An indentured servant signed a legal document called an indenture, agreeing to work for a landowner for a term of four to seven years. The landowner, also called the master, paid the servant's passage from England to the colony and provided food and a place for the servant to sleep. In exchange, the servant essentially belonged to the master for the entire term. For example, if it suited the master, he could sell a servant's indenture to another landowner.

Of the thousands of people who came to the Maryland and Virginia colonies in the seventeenth century, 70 to 85 percent either came as indentured servants or signed indenture papers shortly after their arrival. Most were between the ages of fifteen and twenty-nine, although some were younger. (Younger children had to serve a longer period of time, sometimes as much as twelve years, before they were freed.) Upon completion of an indenture, masters had to give servants their freedom dues: an ax, two farm tools (a hoe, for example), three barrels of corn, and a new suit of clothes. The government also gave servants the right to acquire 50 acres (20 hectares) of their own land.

As Luckenbach explained, "These servants did everything that slaves [did] later," when slavery became more widespread. "The seventeenth century was a hard time even if you were not an indentured servant. But it was particularly bad for indentured servants." They hauled water, butchered hogs and cattle, and hoed tobacco. They hung heavy bundles of tobacco in drying sheds and moved hogsheads—large casks that, when filled with dried tobacco leaves, weighed about 400 pounds (180 kilograms) each. They erected fences and helped build shelters, some for drying tobacco and some for use as homes.

In short, indentured servants did any job the master demanded. And if they died before their term of service ended, their remains met with whatever fate their master chose. At times, masters "treated their dead servants like a waste product," said Luckenbach. In fact, in 1661 Virginia enacted a law that prohibited the inappropriate burial of servants. Similar laws were considered in Maryland. The only reason such laws would have been discussed would be in response to an existing problem.

THE EARLY COLONIAL PLANTATION WORKFORCE included many indentured servants. They signed a document, called an indenture (above), that committed them to work for a landowner for a fixed number of years.

WORKING ON A PLANTATION was physically challenging. Indentured servants routinely carried heavy loads (*left*). Shoes like these (*below*) would've been typical of those worn by indentured servants of the mid-seventeenth century.

To help evaluate his theory about the origins of the skeleton in Neale's cellar, Luckenbach asked Doug Owsley to examine the bones. Using his standard procedures, Owsley determined they belonged to a male who had died when he was about fifteen to sixteen years old. The shape of the boy's skull was similar to skulls of other seventeenth-century English colonists. Measurement of the leg bones revealed that he had been 5 feet 2 inches tall (1.6 m). He wasn't fully grown when he died, though: his arm and leg bone epiphyses were not yet fused.

Next, Owsley searched for clues that might confirm or disprove Luckenbach's suspicion that the boy was a servant. If he had been a servant, he had lived a life very different from most modern American teens. He would have worked at hard labor from before dawn until after dark. Indeed, according to Owsley, "The boy's bones told a story of a short, hard life. Although he was

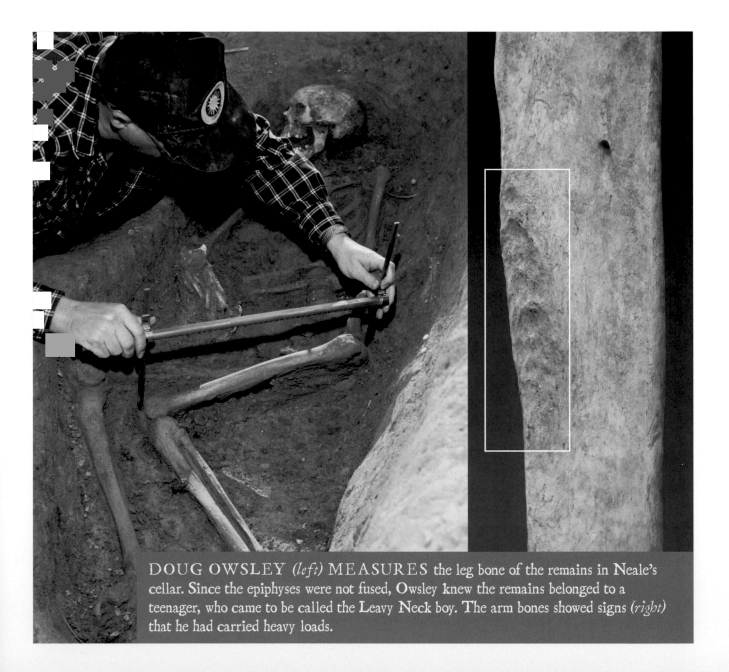

DOUG OWSLEY *(left)* MEASURES the leg bone of the remains in Neale's cellar. Since the epiphyses were not fused, Owsley knew the remains belonged to a teenager, who came to be called the Leavy Neck boy. The arm bones showed signs *(right)* that he had carried heavy loads.

a boy, he did a man's worth of work." The muscle attachment areas on the boy's shoulder bones and humeri were sharply defined, proof that he'd done serious physical labor on a daily basis. He had carried heavy objects, perhaps buckets of water or heavy bundles of tobacco. He'd probably chopped logs for firewood and used a hoe. Perhaps he had moved hogsheads of tobacco. At some point, he had cracked his right elbow against something hard enough to fracture it. The break had healed before his death.

Many of the vertebrae in the boy's lower back had shallow, concave features called Schmorl's depressions. Schmorl's depressions are caused when the spine is compressed by some sort of trauma—for example, lifting heavy objects or twisting the back. (Schmorl's depressions are often seen in modern weight lifters and gymnasts.) At the very least, the teenager in Neale's cellar had, at times, a sore back.

This bone evidence led Owsley to agree with Luckenbach's theory that the boy was an indentured servant. "Indentured servants were often robust. They worked endlessly," he observed. "There were few beasts of burden in the Chesapeake at that time. Wagons with wheels were rare too. When an indentured servant moved or hauled something, it was carried on his or her back." The teenager's bones showed it.

As Luckenbach had observed, the circumstances of the burial pointed toward indentured servitude too. "If servants die you have to bury them. Burial costs the master money," said Owsley. A secret basement burial would have spared Neale the expense of a public one.

It might also have saved him another kind of trouble. Some masters abused their indentured servants, either by mistreating them or by working them to death. A public burial might have given government officials the opportunity to inspect the remains—a situation an abusive master would want to avoid. Had the boy in Neale's basement been mistreated? Only further examination in the laboratory would reveal if abuse might have been a factor that led to a secret basement burial.

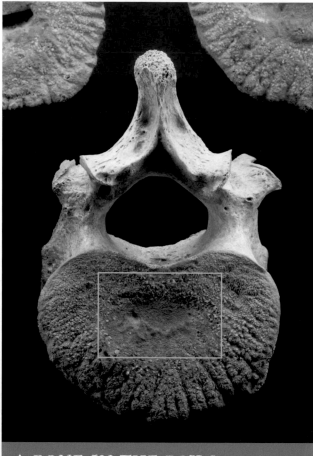

A BONE IN THE BOY'S lower back held a Schmorl's depression, suggesting he may have severely strained his back at some time.

Suspicious Causes

Close study of the boy's skeleton at the Smithsonian Institution showed that his health and general well-being had been neglected for some time. His right humerus had a healed fracture near the elbow. A rib and two leg bones had formations of abnormal bone, and some of the boy's vertebrae exhibited an unusual amount of bone destruction. Owsley had seen these conditions in the bones of people who were known to have suffered from tuberculosis, a disease that infects the lungs and sometimes the skeleton. Tuberculosis often enters the spine. The Leavy Neck boy's bones may reflect the early signs of tuberculosis.

The boy's teeth were in atrocious condition as well. Of the thirty teeth that were present, nineteen had cavities—three large enough to have completely destroyed the crown. Five teeth in the upper jaw and two in the lower had been badly infected. To have left signs in the jawbone, these pus-filled infections must have been ongoing for many weeks, probably months. The teeth, even more than his other ailments, must have caused the young man a great deal of pain. In fact, the infection that resulted from the terrible abscesses around the boy's teeth probably spread throughout the

TUBERCULOSIS OF THE SPINE (*shown here*) can deform the backbone enough to prevent sitting or standing. This spine is from a twelve-year-old colonial boy who died of tuberculosis. Owsley believes that Leavy Neck boy's remains show the early stages of spinal tuberculosis.

boy's body and poisoned his blood. Given the presence of these infections and the possibility of tuberculosis, it seems likely that the boy would have been in a weakened state. He probably found accomplishing a full day's work—something that an indentured servant would have been expected to do—difficult, if not impossible. And that, Owsley theorized, may have been a factor that led to the boy's death.

As the laboratory examination of the skeleton continued, Owsley and Kari Bruwelheide noticed two fractured bones in the right arm. One fracture was in one of several hand bones called the metacarpals. The break was in the area of the bone close to the boy's wrist. The other fracture was in the radius, the thicker of a person's two lower arm bones. The fracture in the radius was at the end closest to the wrist, and it directly lined up with the fracture in the metacarpal bone. Because of this alignment of the two fractures, Owsley knew that they had occurred at the same time. Neither fracture showed any signs of healing, an indication that they occurred near or at the time of death.

STUDIES OF THE BOY'S SKULL revealed more information about his luckless life. Most of his teeth had cavities.

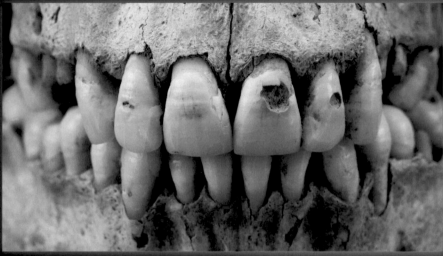

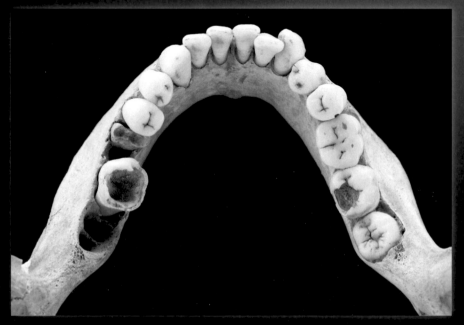

OWSLEY'S CAREFUL STUDY told more about Leavy Neck boy's life. In addition to bad teeth and tuberculosis, he'd suffered from fractures in his hand and in part of the arm bone called the radius (*below*).

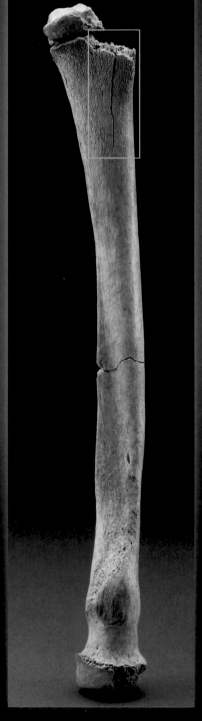

THE HUGE PITS in Leavy Neck boy's teeth (*top and middle*) must have caused him considerable pain and have affected his ability to eat. Pus-filled infections attacked other teeth in his jaw (*bottom*).

BUT WHAT OF THE POTTERY SHERD on Leavy Neck boy's chest? Speculation is that it was used as a shovel to dig the shallow grave into which the boy was pitched.

This type of fracture is consistent with breaks that occur as the result of a blow with a blunt object—a thick stick, for example. Might someone have been angry that the boy wasn't doing a full day's work and hit him to make him work harder? Owsley suspects that the boy was mistreated in this way. "Somehow, someone got carried away and an altercation got out of hand." He speculates that the boy died as a result.

Another look at the circumstances of the boy's burial supports this theory. Owsley reexamined the sherds of the large milk pan under a low level of magnification. He found that the broken edges of the smaller pieces of the milk pan were sharp and jagged, the way a piece of broken ceramic normally appears. The edges of the large sherd, the one that was believed to have been used to cram the boy's body into the grave, were rounded, as if they'd been polished smoother. "I'm absolutely certain this large sherd was used as a digging tool," Owsley stated. "Someone grabbed the sherd with both hands and used the broken edge to dig the pit to hide the body. He or she dug through the trash and then into the floor and part of the cellar wall. The formerly sharp edges of the sherd became rounded with the scraping. There is no other reason for this kind of shaping."

The act of grabbing whatever means were at hand to dig the grave rather than taking the time to get and use a proper tool indicates that the person or people who buried the boy's body did so in haste and secrecy. The clandestine circumstances of the burial further support this scenario. Had the boy died merely as the result of a farm accident, there would have been no reason to hide his death or his burial, other than to avoid burial costs. Together, the forensic clues have led Owsley to believe that the boy died of suspicious causes.

The Leavy Neck boy's carbon-13 isotope value was –19.39, indicating that he hadn't lived in America for a long time before he died. Many of his health problems may have originated in England. If so, his life there must have been difficult as well. On his long journey to the colonies, had the boy dreamed of opportunity—maybe of someday owning his own land? Life as an indentured servant would have filled his days with endless work and demanding chores, leaving little time for dreams. The boy's early death ended them completely.

Chapter Six

THE LUXURY OF LEAD

A VERY DIFFERENT BURIAL, ALSO FOUND IN MARYLAND, has helped archaeologists decipher the story of a colonial family whose lives bore little resemblance to that of the boy found in the Leavy Neck basement. This grave, excavated beneath the foundation of a chapel in St. Mary's City, turned out to be among colonial America's most unique resting places. As archaeologist Henry Miller explained, "The chapel, a solid brick structure dedicated to Catholic worship, could *not* have been built anywhere else in the English-speaking world during colonial times."

As the director of research at Historic St. Mary's City, a re-creation of a colonial settlement, Miller has spent years studying the unusual place Maryland holds in the religious history of the United States. Modern Americans know the United States as a nation of religious freedom. The Constitution protects the right of every individual to practice religion according to personal choice, not law. Centuries ago, however, the first English settlements in America did not allow this freedom, nor did England itself. By law, a branch of Christianity called the Church of England, also known as the Anglican Church, was the nation's official religion. Accordingly, most English people belonged to this church. Some, however, followed other religions, such as Roman Catholicism. Because the law forbade these religions, their followers often had to worship in secret to avoid being harassed, imprisoned, or even killed. It was against the law to build a Roman Catholic church in England or its colonies.

The colony of Maryland was founded in 1634 by a man who was determined to create a safe haven for English Catholics. Cecil Calvert, also known as Lord Baltimore, received a charter from King Charles I to establish a colony on land purchased from the Yaocomaco people. The new colony was named in honor of

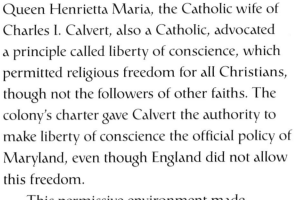

Queen Henrietta Maria, the Catholic wife of Charles I. Calvert, also a Catholic, advocated a principle called liberty of conscience, which permitted religious freedom for all Christians, though not the followers of other faiths. The colony's charter gave Calvert the authority to make liberty of conscience the official policy of Maryland, even though England did not allow this freedom.

This permissive environment made Maryland unique in colonial times. As such, it attracted settlers of many Christian faiths, including Catholics. Among them was a group of priests who built a brick chapel in St. Mary's City in about 1667. The chapel served as a house of worship for many years. But in 1689, a revolution in the colony removed the Calvert family from power and ended religious freedom in Maryland. The government center was moved away from St. Mary's City, and in 1695 Providence—later renamed Annapolis—became the colony's new capital. In 1704, by government order, the chapel doors were locked forever. Later, Catholic priests dismantled its walls and carted the bricks away to be used elsewhere. Only the chapel's sturdy brick foundation, which lay beneath the surface of the ground, remained.

Slowly, as years passed, more soil accumulated over the chapel's foundation. Farmers planted tobacco, corn, and beans in the soil. Eventually, all traces of the

CECIL CALVERT (*above*) never set foot in Maryland, but as Lord Baltimore he used his influence to protect and guide the colony. St. Mary's City become the hub of the colony. More than three hundred years later, archaeologists (*below*) prepare to excavate a broad field where the city's chapel once stood.

foundation were hidden from sight. In fact, almost all traces of St. Mary's City disappeared as well. The surface of the ground gave no hint that anyone had ever lived there.

Nor did the historical record offer many helpful clues to Henry Miller and his team of scientists when they began their work during the early 1980s. "There are no historical documents of the city. No maps. No good written descriptions," Miller explained. "We had to rely on archaeology."

Fortunately, careful scientific investigation proved to be enough. Miller, chief archaeologist Tim Riordan, and the many scientists who have worked with them since excavations began have found thousands of artifacts and the foundations of many of the settlement's buildings, including the brick chapel. They also found a large cemetery that surrounded the chapel's foundation. Their discoveries have revealed many details of seventeenth-century colonial daily life and death. But one of their finds was as unique as the Maryland colony itself.

A Stupendous Find

In the fall of 1990, Stephanie Bandy and Molly Quast, two archaeologists on Riordan's crew, were excavating inside the foundation of the St. Mary's brick chapel, beneath an area where the chapel's floor had been. "[When we scraped the subsoil,] there was a detectable feature on the surface of the soil . . . , but it wasn't a normal grave shaft. It was obviously bigger," Bandy recalled.

Suddenly, her trowel hit something hard. "I think it's a big rock," she called to Tim Riordan. It wasn't long before she realized that she was mistaken. "As soon as we exposed the edge [of the object], we could tell it was shaped like a coffin," she recalled. As she cleared away more soil, the team saw that the object wasn't made of wood. Bandy's discovery turned out to be something no one had expected: a metal coffin.

Miller and Riordan weren't surprised that the team had found a grave inside the chapel. In England burying the bodies of church members beneath the floor of a church or a chapel was a common practice, especially among wealthy people. (It cost more money to be buried inside the church than outside, so only the wealthy could afford such a luxury.) With this knowledge in mind, before the excavation began, Miller and Riordan had asked geophysicist Bruce Bevan to survey the area with ground-penetrating radar (GPR), a scientific technique used to detect and pinpoint the location of buried objects.

MOLLY QUAST (*left*) continues to uncover the first lead coffin as Stephanie Bandy (*right*) watches.

Bevan dragged the GPR equipment across the land surface around and within the chapel's foundation. The equipment sent pulses of radio waves–waves made by electric and magnetic energy–into the ground. Solid objects buried beneath the surface reflect radio waves back toward the surface, much like the way a mirror reflects the rays of light from a flashlight. An antenna attached to the GPR equipment transmits the radio waves to a receiver. A computer translates them into a regular pattern of lines, called an echo, on a monitor. A solid buried object disrupts the pattern and creates a group of zigzagging lines.

Although GPR cannot determine what a buried object is, Miller and Riordan hoped to learn the extent of the chapel's foundation and if any large objects lay buried beneath the floor. Indeed, the GPR echoes revealed a brick foundation that was 3 feet (1 m) thick and that extended 5 feet (1.5 m) under the ground–sufficiently massive to support a tall, permanent building. The foundation had been built in the shape of a cross, a symbol of Christianity often used for a church's foundation.

THE FOUNDATION OF ST. MARY'S chapel was in the shape of a Christian cross.

The GPR also produced a mysterious echo beneath the chapel's floor. This echo, which came from an area in one of the arms of the cross, was even stronger than the foundation's echo. When Bandy began digging in that spot, she'd had no idea what to expect. A big rock was a likely possibility—but a metal coffin was not.

Because the tip of Bandy's trowel had scraped the coffin and left a tiny mark, Miller and Riordan knew the coffin had to be made of a soft metal called lead. In England only royalty or very wealthy people were buried in lead coffins. And in seventeenth-century America, lead coffins were extremely rare. The person buried here must have been someone important. To prevent damage to the coffin, Bandy set aside her trowel. "We used paintbrushes and even a pair of gloves to brush the last bit of the dirt off the top of the coffin," she recalled.

Further excavation led to more surprises—two other lead coffins, one buried on each side of the first. One coffin was larger. The other was big enough only to hold a baby or small child. Miller and Riordan could scarcely believe it: three lead coffins!

The entire team was eager to find out what the coffins contained, but they had to wait. Because the lead coffins appeared to have been undisturbed for

THE THREE LEAD COFFINS (*above*)—one large, one medium-sized, and one small—were mapped and photographed in situ before Project Lead Coffins could begin. The project enlisted the help of dozens of specialists. The planning took two years to complete. A drawing (*below*) shows the location of the many graves buried beneath the chapel.

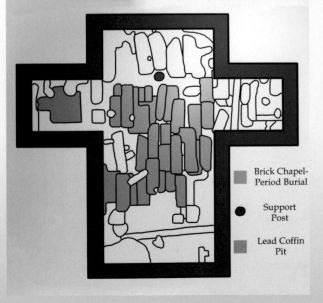

■ Brick Chapel-Period Burial

● Support Post

■ Lead Coffin Pit

centuries, they could provide historians and scientists with an unprecedented opportunity to learn more about seventeenth-century people, their burial customs, and even their environment. For example, if the coffins had been tightly sealed when they were buried and had remained so, they might still contain seventeenth-century air! Scientists could analyze that air and compare it to modern air to discover how the atmosphere had changed over the centuries.

To preserve every bit of evidence that the site might contain, Miller and Riordan had to make a detailed excavation plan, which would require a great deal of thought and the cooperation of many historians and scientists. To leave the coffins unprotected during that time was unthinkable. Television stations and newspapers had widely reported the team's amazing find. "We were concerned about someone sneaking out to the field and digging down to the coffins," explained Tim Riordan. To keep them safe, "we exposed [half of] the top of the coffins and a couple of inches down on each side . . . to make sure that it was just three coffins that were there. We photographed and mapped them and then filled [the grave shaft] back in," explained Stephanie Bandy. Then they covered the backfilled grave shaft with sheets of tin topped with a thick layer of soil.

With the discovery securely protected, Riordan and Miller started planning Project Lead Coffins, a scientific study that would examine the coffins and their contents. They assembled a team of almost one hundred members, including historians, many types of scientists, medical personnel, and photographers.

Over the next two years, as the team researched and developed their strategy,

TO LEARN MORE about lead coffins, the team was allowed to analyze the only other colonial lead coffins known to come from roughly the same period.

historians found a useful clue—a document that described the opening of the only other lead coffins ever found in North America. These two coffins had been buried in an underground vault in the cemetery at Trinity Episcopal Church, also located in St. Mary's City. In 1799 a group of medical students had entered the vault and opened the coffins to study the remains within.

Modern historians believed the coffins contained the remains of Sir Lionel Copely, the first royal governor of Maryland, and his wife, Anne. Both had died in 1693. With permission from Trinity Episcopal Church, the team reopened the Copely vault and examined the two coffins and their contents. They noted how the coffins had been constructed, gathered forensic evidence, and took samples for later isotope analyses that enabled them to confirm the identities of the occupants. This information helped the team to develop a scientifically thorough strategy for excavating and opening the three recently discovered lead coffins.

THE COFFINS HELD the remains of Sir Lionel and Anne Copley, who both died in 1693. Before her body was buried, Anne Copely's skull had been cut open by a saw (*see slanted cut on the side of the skull*). This was done to insert the materials used to embalm, or preserve, her body.

By August 1992, every step of the process had been meticulously planned. Each scientist had a specific role and knew when to collect the samples he or she needed from the grave shaft, the soil, and the coffins. "We had to ensure that one scientist's evidence collection didn't mess up the data for another," recalled Miller. Project Lead Coffins was about to move into action.

Wrapped in Lead

The archaeologists began the excavation by removing backfilled soil to expose the head ends of the three coffins. They were interested not just in the coffins but also in the wall of undisturbed soil left behind after the backfill had been removed. This soil became the object of investigation of geologist Gerald Johnson. Johnson specializes in stratigraphy, a branch of geology that deals with understanding how soil and rock layers and the features found within them are arranged. It explains the order in which layers and features form and how they change when the soil is disturbed. Stratigraphy can provide critical information about the timing and nature of such changes, helping archaeologists to analyze their findings.

The stratigraphy of the undisturbed wall of soil told Johnson an interesting story. He clearly saw the outline of a grave shaft that had been dug wide enough for the two large coffins to be buried in it side by side and at the same depth. That meant they had been buried at the same time. But changes in the soil's color and texture also told Johnson that sometime after that burial, this large grave shaft had been disturbed. The shape of the disturbed area cut down directly through the soil that had been used to fill the large shaft. The tiny coffin lay at the bottom of the disturbed area. Thus Johnson could tell that this tiny coffin had been buried after the two large coffins.

The next step was to attempt to retrieve an air sample from the coffins, a tricky undertaking. Opening a coffin would immediately corrupt the air it contained. Without the correct preparation, a drill or any other instrument inserted into the coffin would break the coffin's airtight seal and let modern air enter the coffin. Nor could the team drill

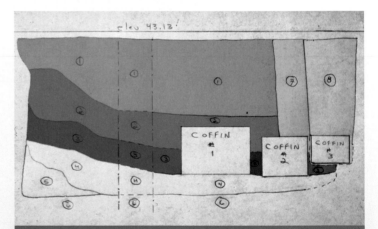

THIS CROSS-SECTION is a diagram of the stratigraphy of the grave shafts and the surrounding soils. To bury the two large coffins, the diggers dug a big pit. They put coffin 1 and coffin 2 in it. These coffins were covered with soil layer 3, then layer 2, and finally layer 1. When the small coffin was buried, a pit was dug through layers 1 and 2 until diggers hit the middle coffin. It and the small coffin were covered by soil layer 7. Sometime later, workers apparently dug up the small coffin, wrapped it in lead, and returned it to the grave pit. Layer 8 is from this second burial.

a hole into a random part of a coffin to obtain a sample. The tool might damage the human remains inside. Before proceeding further, the team had to know exactly how these coffins were constructed and where the remains lay. In other words, they needed a way to see inside the coffins without opening them.

An X-ray is one of the first tools that scientists use in such a situation. In this case, that wouldn't be possible because conventional X-rays can't penetrate lead. Fortunately, the team had anticipated and solved this problem during their planning period by building a small lead coffin for testing purposes. Nuclear physicist Mark Moore experimented with techniques similar to X-rays to find one that could see through lead. The experiments showed that another type of ray, called a gamma ray, easily penetrated the experimental coffin's lead sides.

Like X-rays, gamma rays can be used to create an image. Based on successful trials with the experimental coffin, the team decided to examine the project's coffins with

THE LEAD COFFINS AT ST. MARY'S were scanned with special waves of colored light (*above*). The colored lights have different wavelengths. They can be used to bring out details or stains that are otherwise invisible. The team was looking for special markings, surface treatments on the coffins, and cracks in the lead. None were found.

this technique. In small, measured amounts, gamma rays are helpful in treating certain kinds of cancer. But uncontrolled amounts are very dangerous—they can cause serious illnesses. To protect people from this risk, Maryland state inspectors required the team to build a protective wall around the coffins before they used the gamma rays. The safety wall contained more than six hundred large sacks of sand.

Next, the team put special photographic paper along one side of the head end of each coffin. The instrument that produced the gamma rays was placed on the other side. It directed a short burst of gamma rays toward each coffin. Different materials—for example, lead, wood, or bone—absorb different amounts of gamma rays. Lead absorbs a lot of gamma rays. As the coffin absorbed the rays, the lead appeared as a light area on the gamma-ray image, much like a person's bones show brightly on an X-ray image. Air, on the other hand, absorbs few gamma rays. The rays that passed through air-filled spaces inside the coffins created dark areas on the image.

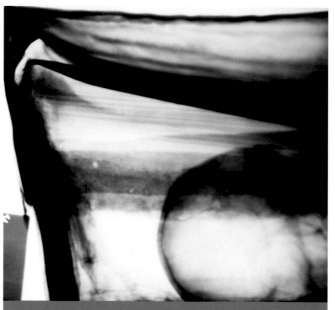

THIS GAMMA-RAY IMAGE (*above*) is of the medium-sized coffin. It shows a skull, the nails and wood grain of the inner coffin, and the lead sheets of the outer coffin. This coffin was no longer airtight.

The images revealed that each set of remains was actually contained in two coffins: the outer lead coffin had been constructed around an inner coffin made of wood. The remains lay inside the wood coffins. Unfortunately, the images also showed that the small and medium-sized coffins did not appear to be sealed tightly shut. In fact, the team could see that the medium-sized coffin's rope handles had rotted, leaving holes that had permitted air to enter the coffin. However, the largest coffin seemed to be tightly sealed. The team hoped that meant it might contain preserved seventeenth-century air.

The team decided to sample the air from the large coffin using a special tool—a drill with an air hose attached—that Mark Moore designed. The gamma-ray image had revealed an empty area in this coffin, so the team knew that drilling into that area wouldn't damage the contents. But sampling the coffin air was still tricky. Even the tiniest hole drilled into the coffin would let modern air inside and contaminate the coffin air. Again, the team was ready with a plan. Using Moore's drill and hose tool, they slowly bored partway into the lead and stopped. The scientists used a vacuum pump to remove all the air from the hose. When the hose was completely air free, they resumed drilling the rest of the way into the coffin.

To make sure the hose was removing only uncontaminated coffin air, the team needed a way to detect any changes in air pressure. Such a change would indicate that the coffin's airtight seal had broken and that outside air was flowing into the coffin. Think of sucking liquid from a juice box. As you drink, you vacuum juice and air from the box. That reduces the air pressure inside the box. The pressure of the air on the outside of the box becomes greater than the air pressure inside, causing the sides of the box to collapse inward. If you then stuck a pin in the box, outside air would flow in through the hole, raising the air pressure inside the box. That increase would be strong enough to push the sides of the box back to their normal position.

THE LARGEST COFFIN was still airtight. The team hoped to be able to get a sample of seventeenth-century air without disturbing the coffin's tight seal.

THE AIR SAMPLING was transferred to a lab for further study.

To measure the air pressure inside the coffin, the scientists connected an air pressure gauge to the air hose. The monitor on the gauge would reflect any changes in the coffin's air pressure. As the team removed air from the coffin, the monitor remained at a constant level, indicating that no modern air from outside the coffin was seeping in. This supported the team's belief that the coffin was airtight. They transferred coffin air into sealed containers, which were sent to a laboratory for analysis.

For a while, the air pressure in the coffin remained stable, but eventually the seal loosened. "The coffin held the seal for about three hours, then it started letting go," said Miller. The pressure gauge monitor showed that outside air—containing oxygen—was seeping in.

Oxygen gas reacts with many substances, including human remains. In 1799, when the medical students unsealed Anne Copely's coffin, they reported that her body, hair, and burial clothing were still well preserved. But as soon as the students opened her coffin, oxygen reacted with her flesh, hair, and clothing, causing ruinous results. The students reported that within a few hours, the cloth and flesh had crumbled to bits. Two hundred years later, when the Project Lead Coffins team reopened the coffin, no traces of fabric remained.

Of course, Miller and Riordan had no intention of allowing the remains inside their lead coffins to disintegrate. During their preparations, they had developed a solution to the oxygen problem. First, the team stopped the inflowing gas. The next step was to replace the oxygen with an inert gas called argon. Inert gases do not react with other substances, so they don't contribute to decomposition.

While the coffins had lain buried below the surface, their contents were the same temperature as the soil surrounding them, about 50 to 60°F (10 to 16°C). As the team excavated, however, the lights they used for visibility had heated the air, causing a temperature increase around the grave shaft of about 10°F (6°C). That increase would have also raised the temperature of the argon. Even though argon is inert, the additional warmth from the gas might have posed a threat to the remains. Again, the team was ready with a solution—but this one didn't require any

THE TEAM DIDN'T WANT DETERIORATION to happen to the lead-coffin people. To avoid any degradation, team members pumped neutral argon gas into the coffins (*above*), which doesn't interact as oxygen can.

TO MAKE THE SOIL PEEL, Gerald Johnson first paints resin onto the soil wall (*above*). After removing the soil peel (*below*), Johnson placed it on a plywood board to support it as he and his colleagues lifted the peel from the grave shaft. The cheese cloth is visible along the edges of the peel.

cutting-edge technology. They simply filled a picnic cooler with ice. Before they pumped the argon gas into the coffins, they channeled it through the cooler, chilling it to the same temperature as the soil that had surrounded the coffins.

Through this method, the team protected the remains in all three coffins from further decomposition. The last step before they removed the soil wall that still surrounded the foot ends of the three coffins was to make a record called a soil peel. Gerald Johnson treated the wall with a sticky substance called resin. Then he smoothed a layer of cheesecloth over the resin, covering the entire exposed soil surface. He applied a coat of resin to the cloth and topped that with another layer of cloth. After the resin dried, Johnson peeled the cloth from the wall. The soil that had formed the face of the wall was stuck to the resin, creating an exact copy of the soil layers. The soil peel was stored in the St. Mary's City laboratory so that it could be consulted if further questions arose concerning the stratigraphy of the grave.

To the Clean Room

In a typical excavation, the next step after exposing remains is to undertake an in situ examination. But nothing was typical about this situation. The size of the grave shaft and the conditions at the site made an in situ examination of the coffins' contents impossible. The coffins would have to be removed from the grave before they were opened.

The team prepared for this step by testing the strength of each coffin to ensure that it could be moved safely. The coffins were scanned with infrared light, a type of light that allows scientists to see how metal retains and loses heat. After heating the coffin surfaces slightly, the scientists watched the metal cool under the infrared light. Areas that contain cracks cool at a different rate than undamaged metal, making the cracks readily visible under infrared light. If the coffins contained cracks, the lifting process could place enough stress on the lead to widen them. The coffins might break into pieces. Fortunately, the infrared light revealed no cracks.

Lifting the lead coffins–the largest weighed almost 1,500 pounds (680 kg)–was a formidable task. Mathematicians used special instruments to calculate the thickness of the lead. From those calculations, they determined each coffin's weight. To raise the coffins in the safest possible way, the team decided to lift them on metal plates, starting with the baby's coffin. Positioned alongside it, a hydraulic jack

MOVING THE LEAD COFFINS was no easy task. The team came up with elaborate methods for lifting them from the site and moving them into the lab.

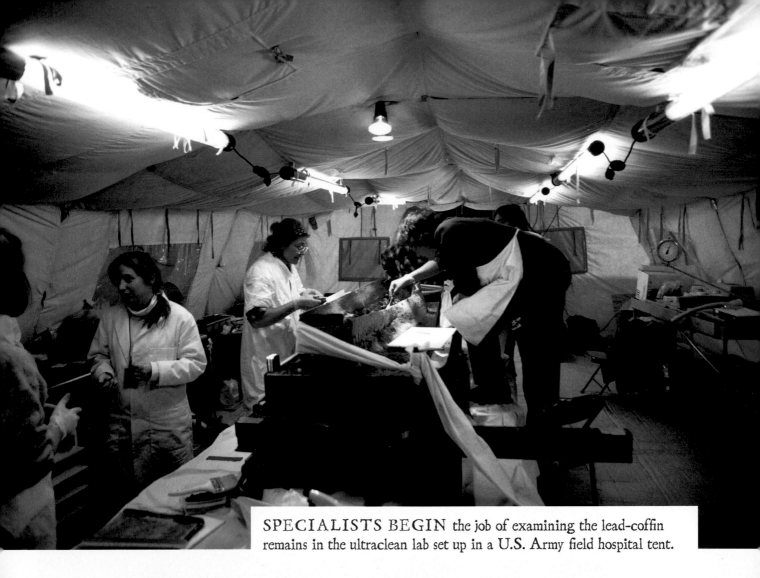

SPECIALISTS BEGIN the job of examining the lead-coffin remains in the ultraclean lab set up in a U.S. Army field hospital tent.

gently pushed a rectangular plate into the soil a few inches below the coffin. The layer of soil between the plate and the coffin served as a cushion. The jack slowly pulled the little coffin away from the medium-sized coffin. A minicrane lifted the plate and coffin up and out of the grave shaft.

As soon as each coffin had been safely lifted from the grave shaft, it was taken to a clean room, a spotlessly clean laboratory area. The clean room at this site was a U.S. Army surgical field tent that had been specially set up in the field near the chapel's foundation. Inside the tent, Doug Owsley, Kari Bruwelheide, archaeological conservators, and medical personnel analyzed and sampled the remains for further scientific analysis. What they found amazed and puzzled them.

Chapter Seven

THE LEAD-COFFIN PEOPLE

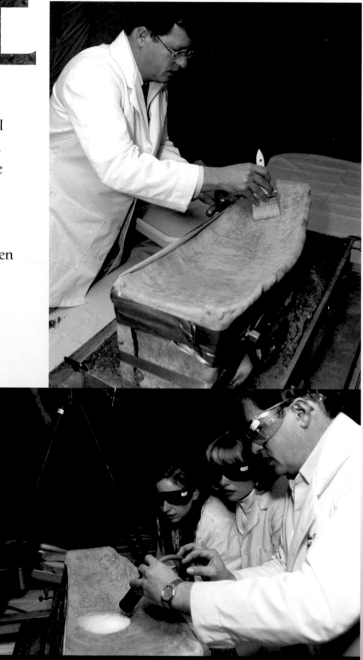

AS THE TEAM HAD SUSPECTED, the small coffin contained the skeleton of a child. In the seventeenth-century Chesapeake area, death was an ever-present fact of life—especially for children, who were particularly vulnerable to disease and starvation. One-fourth of all the children born in Maryland during this period died during the first year of life. Of the survivors, almost half died before they turned twenty. For a child to have four living grandparents was rare. In fact, a colonial child could expect that at least one parent and maybe both would die before that child grew up. As a result of the high death rate, remarriage and stepfamilies were very common.

Most of the lead-coffin child's bones seemed to be in good to excellent condition—a surprise, given that the fragile bones of children often decay rapidly. But the coffin also contained a mystery: the

DOUG OWSLEY CAREFULLY BRUSHES off the lid of the smallest coffin, thought to hold the remains of a child (*top*). He examines the exterior before opening it the first time (*above*).

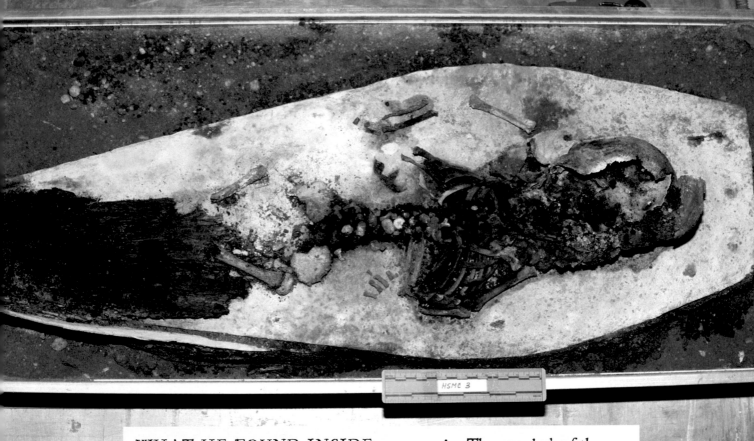

WHAT HE FOUND INSIDE was a surprise. The upper body of the child's skeleton was relatively complete, but the lower portion was missing.

child's lower leg bones and feet were gone. Had they somehow been severed by an injury? Could such an event have been the cause of death?

As Doug Owsley and Kari Bruwelheide investigated further, they saw green stains left by copper shroud pins on the skull, the collarbone, the jaw, and a rib. Then conservators pointed out yet another amazing discovery: tiny fragments of the linen material that the St. Mary's City women had used to shroud the child. (Traditionally, English women prepared the dead for burial.)

Fabric from seventeenth-century colonial burials rarely survives the effects of time and decomposition. Occasionally, however, some fragments do. The lead-coffin linen fragments were most likely preserved by the shroud pins in a fascinating example of the way the circumstances of a burial affect what remains—and does not—centuries later. As Silas Hurry, the director of the archaeology laboratory at St. Mary's City, explained, "Copper is a fairly toxic [poisonous] metal. When there are copper pins in contact with fabric, critters [insects, fungi, and microscopic organisms] don't eat the cloth in contact with the copper. As the copper corrodes, or decays, the fabric strands around it are preserved, almost like a fossil."

Wondering how old the child had been, Bruwelheide turned her attention to the cranium. Children's smaller craniums can also offer detailed information about a person's age at the time of death. An adult human skull is made of twenty-eight bones, which includes the six ear bones. The bones of an adult's cranium are solidly fused together. At birth, however, an infant's skull needs to have a degree of flexibility to pass through the birth canal without being damaged. Further flexibility is needed as the infant grows and the skull changes. Thus the bones of an infant's cranium are not fused together. Instead, fibrous joints called sutures fill the spaces between the bones.

Sutures appear on the cranium as zigzagging lines. They're easy to see on the skulls of children, teenagers, and young adults. As a person gets older, the suture lines often become more intricate. This holds the cranium's bones more tightly together. Some of the sutures on the skull of an elderly person may fade and disappear completely. Thus a forensic anthropologist can study sutures to estimate a person's age. In this way, Bruwelheide determined that the child was very young—no more than a toddler. But how young?

KARI BRUWELHEIDE (*above*) examines the child's cranium. She was looking for the zigzagging lines (*below*) that indicate age.

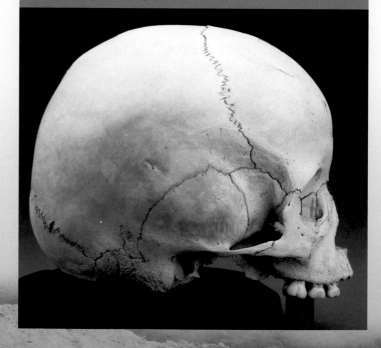

Bruwelheide believed that the teeth might reveal the answer to that question, so she examined the child's mandible, or jaw. She saw that the height of two incisors indicated they had partly grown in while the child was alive. A baby's first incisors usually start to come in when the child is between four and six months old. The rest of the child's teeth had not yet formed. Based on these facts, Bruwelheide estimated the child had been five to six months old at death—only a baby.

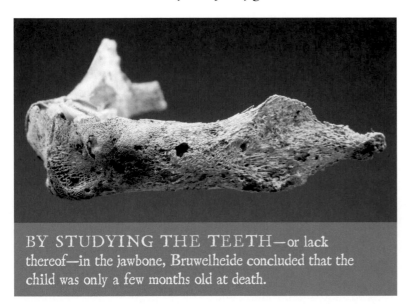

BY STUDYING THE TEETH—or lack thereof—in the jawbone, Bruwelheide concluded that the child was only a few months old at death.

As Owsley and Bruwelheide conducted their examinations, other team members studied the tiny coffin and the rest of its contents. The tiny coffin proved to have been built at a different time than the other two. Three pieces of lead had been used in its manufacture. Careful comparison showed that they "were not leftover scraps from the larger coffins," noted Silas Hurry. "There are hammer marks on the lead. It had served another purpose [perhaps as a tabletop or roof] before it had been turned into a coffin," he added.

An unusual find within the coffin posed a puzzle: a layer of soil partially covered the body when the coffin was opened, while another layer lay beneath the baby's skull and upper body. It's normal to find soil from the grave shaft inside a coffin. The soil enters as the coffin decomposes. But the lead coffin hadn't decomposed. Even though it wasn't airtight, it had no gaps large enough for grave shaft soil to enter.

One of the soil layers consisted of gray soil. The other was brown. So the soils clearly came from different places. Furthermore, both were different from the soil that had filled the grave shaft. Where had they come from—and when?

The team considered a theory that the child may have initially been buried only in the wooden coffin that was found within the lead one. Sometime later, the wooden coffin was dug up, placed into the lead coffin, and reburied. The soil could

THE LAYERS OF SOIL in the baby's coffin show a white thin band. This is the bottom of the lead coffin. Above that is a dark brown layer, on which the baby's body was resting. The grayish soil layer was put over the baby.

have fallen into the wooden coffin during this process. Another possibility was that the soil had been used to prop the child's head and upper body higher in the coffin prior to burial so that grieving family members could more easily see the child when they paid their last respects. Given the two separate soil layers, both theories could have been correct.

To gather more data, the team sent samples scraped from the surface of each layer to a laboratory for pollen analysis. Pollen, the tiny yellow grains found on the reproductive parts of plants, is produced by different plant species at varying times of the year. Any pollen that was floating in the air at the time the soils were placed in the coffin would have settled onto the surface. Identifying the pollen might therefore help the team determine during what season the soils were placed into the infant's coffin.

Gerald Kelso, the team's palynologist, or pollen specialist, found that the two soils contained different types of pollen. One soil had pollen from an oak tree. The other had pine tree pollen. These tree species release their pollen at different times during the spring, suggesting that the soils were placed in the coffin at those times.

Unfortunately, the soil analysis couldn't tell the team exactly where the soils came from or how they entered the coffin. Although this question continues to puzzle the team, they believe they've figured out the answer to an earlier mystery—that of the baby's missing leg and foot bones. Because the coffin wasn't airtight, it must not have been watertight either. Over time, water droplets had seeped into the coffin and dampened the soil. Gravity pulled the water down through the slanted layer of soil to the area where the baby's lower legs and feet lay. The damp conditions caused the lower leg bones and feet to deteriorate and eventually disappear. The upper part of the skeleton remained intact because it wasn't exposed to as much moisture.

Even when a baby's entire skeleton is well preserved, determining whether the child was a boy or a girl is almost impossible. The differences in skulls and pelvic bones that forensic anthropologists rely upon for this purpose generally aren't noticeable until a person has reached the teen years or beyond. That said, Owsley could make an educated guess. The lead-coffin baby had small teeth and a pointed chin. These factors, plus a wide angle in one area of the hip bone, suggested that the baby was more likely to have been a girl than a boy.

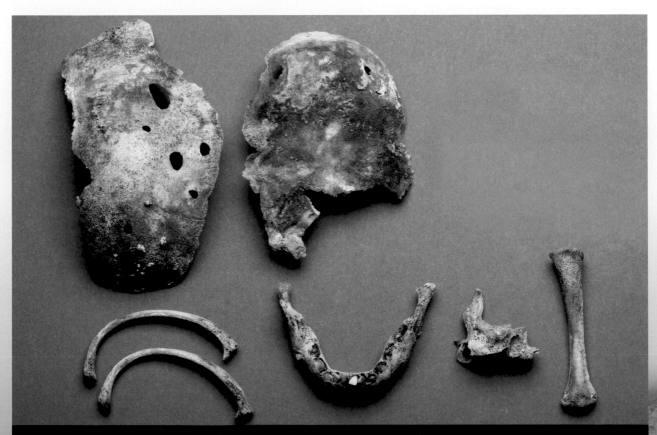

THIS IMAGE SHOWS TWO CRANIUM sections *(top)*, and *(from left to right)* two ribs, the lower jaw, part of the upper jaw, and an arm bone that belonged to the lead-coffin baby.

Could Owsley and Bruwelheide discover why the baby had died? As they examined the baby's cranium, they noticed a number of abnormal holes. Some were very tiny. Others were as large as 0.2 inches (0.6 centimeters). Abnormal holes of this kind are a sign of serious disease. They indicate that the child's bones were not forming properly as she grew.

One condition that causes abnormal holes like the ones found in the lead-coffin baby's cranium is rickets, a disease resulting from lack of vitamin D, calcium, and sunlight. Rickets causes unhealthy bone changes in children. For example, the skull bones become thin, so they break easily. The ends of the ribs become flared—wider than normal. Other bones become soft enough to bend and bow into abnormal shapes. When Owsley and Bruwelheide examined the baby's ribs, they found that the ends were flared exactly as one would expect in a child who suffered from rickets.

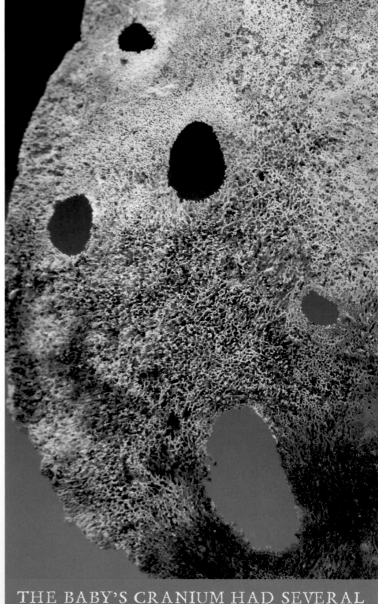

THE BABY'S CRANIUM HAD SEVERAL large holes (*above*). They told researchers that the girl suffered from rickets.

Historical documents show that colonial mothers often kept their babies swaddled, or wrapped tightly in cloth. Swaddling would have prevented the baby's body from absorbing sunlight, which, along with poor nutrition, could cause rickets.

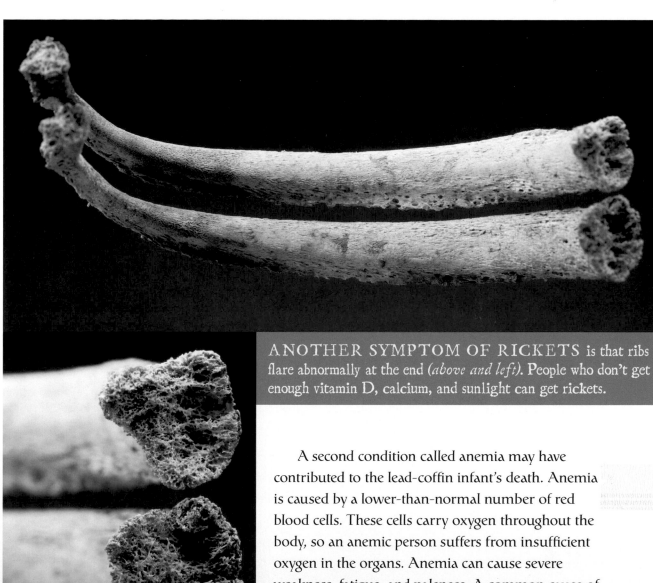

ANOTHER SYMPTOM OF RICKETS is that ribs flare abnormally at the end *(above and left)*. People who don't get enough vitamin D, calcium, and sunlight can get rickets.

A second condition called anemia may have contributed to the lead-coffin infant's death. Anemia is caused by a lower-than-normal number of red blood cells. These cells carry oxygen throughout the body, so an anemic person suffers from insufficient oxygen in the organs. Anemia can cause severe weakness, fatigue, and paleness. A common cause of anemia is a lack of the element iron, found in leafy green vegetables and meat.

In colonial times, doctors believed that people fell ill because their blood had turned bad. Making a cut in the patient's skin to release this supposedly bad blood—a practice called bloodletting—was one way doctors tried to cure sickness. (Modern medical doctors know that removing blood weakens an ill person.) If the lead-coffin baby was bled as her illness worsened, as would have been the custom, she would have become sicker. Owsley and Bruwelheide are certain that rickets and possibly anemia led to the little girl's death.

The lead-coffin baby offers clear proof that infants in the colonial Chesapeake were susceptible to many diseases. Given that the baby's family was wealthy—after all, only a wealthy family would be able to bury a child in a lead coffin—it seems likely that they would have spared no expense in her medical care. Even so, by the time she died, the lead-coffin baby was a very sick child and had been so for some time. Her death appears to have been the result of her illnesses.

The Lady of the Manor

The remains in the second lead coffin told the story of a much longer life. The coffin, although better made than the baby's, wasn't perfect. Small nicks in the lead sheeting were caused by errors in cutting. The addition of a small lead extension strip showed that the coffin maker was inexperienced at making lead coffins. That's not surprising, since they were uncommon. The body, however, fit perfectly in the narrow inner coffin made of yellow pine, an indication the occupant had been slender. The wooden coffin lid had cracked and collapsed onto the skeleton, damaging several bones in the pelvis. Traces of dried tissue still clung to the individual's bones, and a fair amount of fine, brown hair covered the skull. Some of the vertebrae showed signs of arthritis. From dental and bone clues, Owsley and Bruwelheide concluded that the remains belonged to a slender woman, about 5 feet 3 inches tall (1.6 m), who had lived to be at least sixty years old.

Three discoveries confirmed that the women who prepared this body for burial had treated it with great respect. Remnant strands of linen were still wrapped around some corroded, green pins, proving that she had been shrouded.

THIS IMAGE, GREATLY ENLARGED, shows the texture of the ribbon that had been wrapped around the lead-coffin lady's wrists.

THE SECOND LEAD COFFIN *(above)*
contained the remains of a grown woman. Her skull was
still covered in hair *(above right)*. Owsley and colleague
Tim Riordan study the way the body was treated before
burial *(right)*.

The other two pieces of evidence were far more unusual. A silk ribbon, tied neatly in a bow around the lady's wrists, held her hands in place across her waist. And sprigs of rosemary, a strong-smelling herb, were strewn over her body. "Rosemary was an herb the English used for remembrance," explained Henry Miller, noting that this custom is mentioned by the character of Ophelia in William Shakespeare's famous play *Hamlet*, written in about 1599. Traditionally, Europeans and the English placed cuttings of rosemary at weddings and funerals as a reminder to keep people in one's memories. "Seeing this ritual continue on this side of the Atlantic shows how the colonists were trying to follow English tradition," Miller added.

As Owsley and Bruwelheide studied the woman's bones, they noticed that many had lost mass and become thin. Thinned bones like these are a sign of a condition called osteoporosis, which results from a lack of calcium in the diet. The bones of people with osteoporosis become brittle and break easily.

"Much of the time during the last years of her life, she was in a lot of pain," said Owsley. "And she walked with a limp." A quick glance at the lady's right femur was all Owsley needed to make these deductions. The shaft of the bone was enlarged and badly deformed. "Several years before she died, she fractured her femur," he explained. When the bone broke, the lower half of the bone twisted and shifted upward. The pain would have been agonizing.

When a person breaks a leg bone in this way in modern times, a surgeon realigns the bone correctly and braces it with a metal plate, which is fastened to the bone with screws. A system of cables and pulleys known as traction may be used to maintain the leg in an elevated, immobile position for a short time as the bone

THESE CROSS-SECTIONS SHOW that the bones of the lead-coffin woman (*right*) were far thinner and more fragile than those of the person in the largest lead coffin (*left*).

THE LEAD-COFFIN WOMAN'S LEG BONES showed that she had broken her upper leg bone and that it had not healed well. Because of the break, her legs were of different lengths, and she likely had a painful limp. The large hole (*detail, right*) is due to ongoing infection in the bone that occurred even after the fracture had mended. Pus would have drained from the infected area through the smaller holes above.

begins to heal. In colonial times, the best that could be done was to hold the leg in place with a wood splint while the patient rested in bed for several weeks.

In the case of the lead-coffin lady, new bone had grown in her femur at the area of the break, fusing the two broken pieces together. That's how Owsley could tell that she had broken the bone several years before her death. Bone measurements confirmed what was easily visible: her right leg was about 1 inch (2.5 cm) shorter than the left—more than enough difference to cause a limp. An irregular bony growth on the femur, near the area of the fracture, told Owsley that the broken bone was also plagued with an ongoing infection that occasionally flared up, causing the lady additional pain.

But the leg wasn't her only problem. She'd lost twenty teeth by the time of her death. Many of her nine remaining teeth had decayed. Others were worn down to the gum line. The positions of the remaining teeth were such that when she chewed, none of them would have closed together. Furthermore, the roots of these teeth barely held them in place, so it's likely that she could only eat very soft foods.

Despite these problems, Owsley did find evidence that the woman had tried to take care of her teeth or at least to make them look better. Her lower teeth—even below the gum line—were marred by a deep hollow that Owsley recognized as evidence of a common method of tooth cleaning. Practitioners wrapped a cloth around a finger, dipped it into a gritty paste, and scrubbed the cloth across the surface of the teeth.

Unfortunately, the colonial formula for tooth polish was a recipe for disaster. The ingredients of the paste were vinegar, salt, and tobacco ashes, which contain microscopic particles of an element called silicon. Although the intent

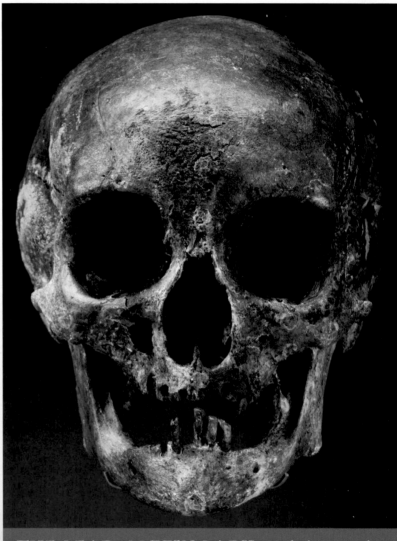

THE LEAD-COFFIN LADY only had nine teeth left when she died.

was to make teeth appear sparkling white, the salt grains, the gritty silicon particles, and the acidic vinegar actually wore away the enamel of a person's teeth. Over time, the scrubbing created a visible worn area across the teeth. Sometimes this furrow was deep

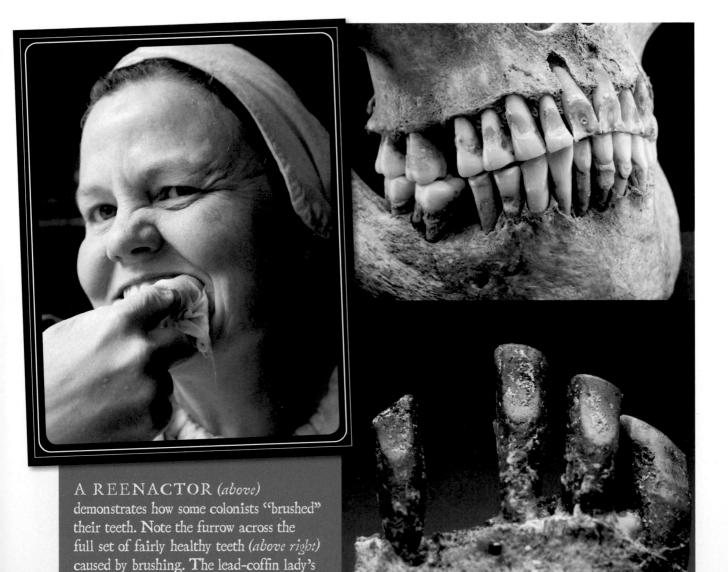

A REENACTOR *(above)* demonstrates how some colonists "brushed" their teeth. Note the furrow across the full set of fairly healthy teeth *(above right)* caused by brushing. The lead-coffin lady's teeth *(right)* have the same kind of furrow.

enough to expose the pulp. This treatment undoubtedly contributed to the lead-coffin lady's tooth loss. Had she lived a few years longer, all of her teeth would have fallen out.

In her final years, the lady would have been malnourished because she was unable to eat a variety of healthy foods. It's likely that she was often inactive and at times bedridden due to the chronic infection and pain in her leg. As if the suffering from these ailments wasn't enough, laboratory tests revealed something even more disturbing.

The Lady in the Laboratory

Laboratory analyses of the lead-coffin lady's hair, carried out by Mark Moore at Pennsylvania State University, yielded more information about her life and death. All hair contains trace elements, minerals found in small amounts. Most of these elements—zinc and iron, for example—help us stay healthy. The amount of trace elements in the foods and liquids that people eat and drink can affect the levels found in their hair. A strand of hair, from scalp to end, therefore contains a record of the trace elements that the growing hair has absorbed from a person's body.

As a nuclear physicist, Moore knew how to use a device called a nuclear reactor to analyze the trace elements in a strand of hair. (Much larger nuclear reactors are typically used as an energy source for the generation of electricity.) Scientists clipped the woman's hair sample into short lengths and placed them inside the reactor, starting with the segments that grew closest to the woman's scalp. The reactor then bombarded the hair with neutrons.

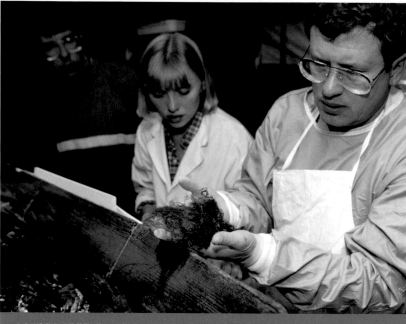

OWSLEY REMOVES some of the lead-coffin lady's hair for further analysis.

Trace elements that are bombarded with neutrons become radioactive. Radioactive materials emit certain kinds of rays. Each trace element, no matter how small the amount, can be identified by measuring the type and amount of rays it emits.

Moore was astounded to learn that the woman's hair contained very high levels of the element arsenic, a deadly poison! And the level of arsenic increased the closer the hair segment was to her scalp. According to Henry Miller, that means "in the months before she died, she was consuming more and more arsenic."

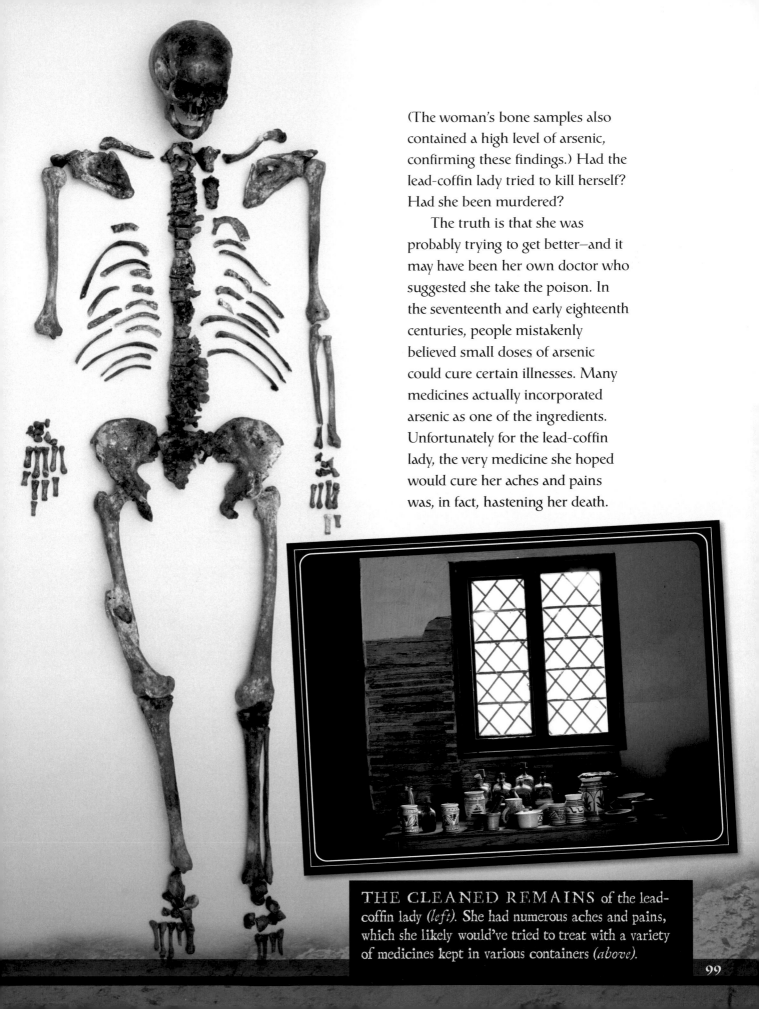

(The woman's bone samples also contained a high level of arsenic, confirming these findings.) Had the lead-coffin lady tried to kill herself? Had she been murdered?

The truth is that she was probably trying to get better—and it may have been her own doctor who suggested she take the poison. In the seventeenth and early eighteenth centuries, people mistakenly believed small doses of arsenic could cure certain illnesses. Many medicines actually incorporated arsenic as one of the ingredients. Unfortunately for the lead-coffin lady, the very medicine she hoped would cure her aches and pains was, in fact, hastening her death.

THE CLEANED REMAINS of the lead-coffin lady (*left*). She had numerous aches and pains, which she likely would've tried to treat with a variety of medicines kept in various containers (*above*).

In this case, a poverty-stricken person who had wanted to take the medicine but was unable to afford it would definitely have fared better than she did.

What might this woman's daily life have been like? Unfortunately, as Henry Miller explained, archaeologists and historians have found "little good data about how high status women lived in early Maryland." Still, they know enough for Miller to make an educated guess. As the lady of the house and a relatively wealthy person, she never would have worked in the fields. She did have a buildup of bone at the muscle attachment sites on her upper arms, however. "It's certain that [she was] physically active," Miller continued. "She probably did various household chores, such as cooking, and likely worked in the garden—both female tasks of the period. She may have had a hand in dairying, although milkmaids would [have done] much of that." The life of the Chesapeake's upper class, while far easier than that of those who worked in the fields, wasn't just a life of leisure.

The Man of the House

The largest lead coffin was the heaviest and most finely crafted of the three. Two sheets of lead had been fashioned into hexagonally shaped boxes. One had been placed on top of the other so that they fit together in much the way a shoe box and its lid do. Nails driven through the lead and into the wood coffin held the lead securely in place. The wood coffin inside the lead one was made of several kinds of wood. The lid was so beautifully preserved "you could [still] drive nails into it," said Henry Miller.

THE LEAD-COFFIN MAN WAS ENCASED in a stout wood coffin that was finely made before it was wrapped with lead.

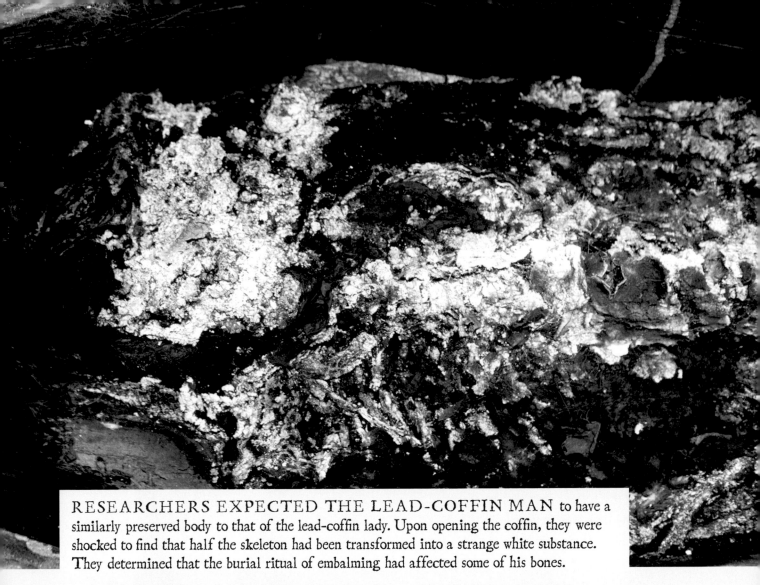

RESEARCHERS EXPECTED THE LEAD-COFFIN MAN to have a similarly preserved body to that of the lead-coffin lady. Upon opening the coffin, they were shocked to find that half the skeleton had been transformed into a strange white substance. They determined that the burial ritual of embalming had affected some of his bones.

During the seventeenth century, when the English buried a husband and wife beside each other, they traditionally placed the husband's grave on the north side of the wife's grave. The large lead coffin was on the north side of the woman's coffin, so the team knew that if the large coffin contained the remains of a man, he may well have been the woman's husband.

No one expected what they actually found inside the coffin, though. "We were shocked!" Miller recalled. "From the waist up, most of the bone had been transformed into a white crystalline material!"

Miller and his team feel certain that the surprising state of the skeleton is a result of embalming. During this burial practice, the organs are removed from inside the body and the skull. When remains were embalmed during the seventeenth century, the empty body and skull were cleaned and filled with a mixture of salt, a white powder called alum, lime (a substance found in certain types of rock), and herbs. This mixture preserved the body by slowing the rate of decomposition.

How did the team link the crystal remains to this practice? Geologists identified the crystals found in the coffin as a mineral called brushite. Brushite forms when elements in salt and alum combine with calcium, one of the elements in bone. The brushite was located in exactly the areas where embalming materials would have been placed. Bones in other areas were unchanged. If the team's analysis is correct, the brushite remains are the earliest evidence of embalming in colonial America.

Fortunately, the rest of the skeleton had not transformed into brushite. "From the waist down, the skeleton was in excellent condition," Henry Miller noted. "Even the toenails were there." These bones, along with teeth found in the coffin, provided Owsley and Bruwelheide with enough evidence to conclude that the remains belonged to a male in his fifties who was probably

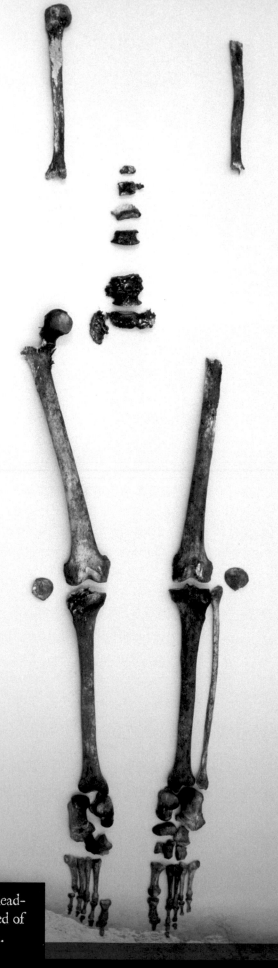

COMPARED TO the lead-coffin lady, not much remained of the lead-coffin man's skeleton.

right handed, about 5 feet 7 inches tall (1.7 m), and–as suggested by the coffin's width–somewhat overweight. His bones showed no evidence that he had worked long hours doing heavy chores. Clearly, like the Captain at Jamestown, the lead-coffin man had been a gentleman of the upper class. Owsley found no signs of debilitating illness, ongoing health problems, or a severe injury. It appeared the man probably died after a short or sudden illness, such as a fever or a heart attack.

He did smoke, however. Owsley puzzled out the facts this way. The man in the grave had seventeen teeth. They showed signs of moderate wear and two small cavities. The teeth are what told Owsley that the man was a smoker. When pipe smokers repeatedly clamp their teeth on a pipestem to hold the pipe in place, the edges of their teeth become worn. The worn areas are called facets. The wear pattern that pipe facets create exactly reflects the curve of a pipe's stem. The lead coffin man's pipe facets proved he was a pipe smoker.

Meanwhile, Tim Riordan had found traces of silk ribbon in the area where the man's neck would have been and around each of his wrists. The man must have worn a burial garment other than a shroud. From historical research, Riordan had learned that toward the end of the seventeenth century, shrouds were often replaced–especially among wealthier people– with a long, shirtlike garment and a cap with a chin strap. The women who prepared the lead-coffin man's body must have thought that he deserved the very best burial garb, yet another indication that he was a person of high status.

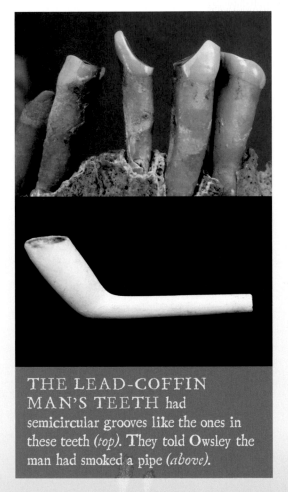

THE LEAD-COFFIN MAN'S TEETH had semicircular grooves like the ones in these teeth *(top)*. They told Owsley the man had smoked a pipe *(above)*.

Although the third coffin and its contents had provided much information, the team's hopes of learning about seventeenth-century air were dashed when Miller received the results of the laboratory tests on the air sample taken before the coffin was opened. The analysis revealed that the sample was indeed very old, but it also contained chemical components not found in pure air. Miller thinks that these chemicals came from the materials used to embalm the man's body. Even worse, the sample also contained small traces of a modern gas that showed that the coffin air had been contaminated before the team sampled it. For these reasons, the team was unable to draw any conclusions from the sample about seventeenth-century air.

While the team knew much more about the lead-coffin people than when they began their examinations, they hoped they could add one more puzzle piece. Would it be possible to find out the identities of the coffin occupants?

Naming the Unnamed

That task became a priority for Lois Green Carr, the historian for Project Lead Coffins and St. Mary's City. As she compiled a list of possible names from historical documents, she kept in mind several facts and theories. Archaeological data told her that the three lead coffins were buried between 1667 and 1704, the dates when the chapel had been used. Since the burials were inside the chapel, the people must have been wealthy Roman Catholics who had been important community members. From Owsley and Bruwelheide's work, Carr knew the sex of each adult and their approximate ages at the time of death. Because the three coffins were buried together, the archaeologists were inclined to believe that the individuals were related. However, the woman's age—at least sixty—ruled her out as the baby's mother.

A piece of data from the laboratory analysis proved especially useful. The carbon-13 value for the lead-coffin man was –17.4. The lead-coffin lady's was –17.1. These two people had lived in Maryland, eating corn as part of their diets, long enough for the carbon-13 content of their bones to change accordingly. Carr therefore eliminated from her list of candidates the names of people who had died shortly after their arrival from England.

Carr focused her search first on men who fit the criteria. This choice was more likely to produce successful results because English men of the seventeenth century, far more often than women, were mentioned in legal documents such as land deeds, business transactions, wills, and government papers. Under the law, married women did not have equal status with men, especially in the area of property ownership. Thus they were seldom mentioned in historical documents, making research about women far more difficult.

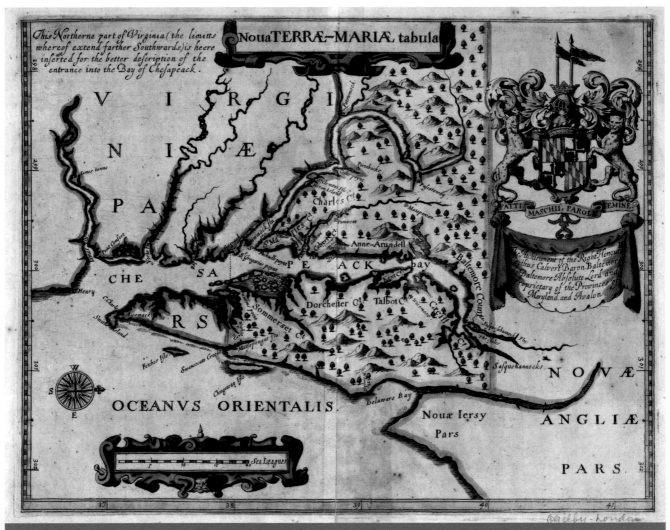

This Northerne part of Virginia (the limitts whereof extend farther Southwards) is heere inserted for the better description of the entrance into the Bay of Chesapeack.

NouaTERRÆ~MARIÆ tabula

THIS MAP DATES FROM 1671, when Cecil Calvert and his half brother Philip were still alive and active. It shows the extent of Maryland (Terrae-Mariae) and includes the Calvert coat of arms, or family symbol. The words on the symbol translate to "Deeds are masculine, words are feminine."

Carr therefore assembled a list of prominent men of seventeenth-century Maryland, including details such as age, the names of wives, when they had arrived in North America, their occupations and community standing, and where and at what time of year they had died. (The small amount of pollen found in the man's coffin indicated that he was buried in the winter, a time when little pollen is floating in the air.) Carr's final list included ten men, but only one, Philip Calvert, perfectly fit all the historical evidence as well as the scientific evidence collected by the Project Lead Coffins's scientists.

Carr's thorough search of the historical record revealed that Philip Calvert was the younger half brother of Cecil Calvert, the founder of the Maryland colony. Philip and his wife, Anne Wolsey Calvert, arrived in St. Mary's City, in 1657. Over the years, he served as the governor, the mayor of St. Mary's City, the chief judge, and the chancellor of the colony—all very powerful positions.

"Philip was a very wealthy man. [The historical record indicates that] his home, a red brick mansion he named St. Peters, was the largest colonial mansion in English America, in 1678. [That makes it] a major building," Henry Miller stated. From a 1682 inventory of Philip's property, Lois Carr discovered that Philip had a personal library of more than one hundred books—one of the largest libraries in colonial Maryland. This wealth alone would have given him a prominent place in St. Mary's City society, but Philip Calvert was clearly respected for his leadership in the community as well. He was therefore a fitting candidate for a lead-coffin burial.

PHILIP CALVERT'S signature on a court document from 1657

While the exact date of Philip's death eluded Carr, she did find a document that narrowed the possibilities to sometime between December 22, 1682, and late January 1683. He was fifty-six years old at the time of his death.

In a will dated 1678, Anne Calvert was left a silver watch. Evidently, Carr concluded, Anne must have been alive then. But Philip and his wife *Jane*—not Anne—signed a deed, or ownership paper, in March 1681. It seemed equally evident to Carr that Anne had died sometime before that date and that Philip had then remarried. His second wife, Jane Sewell, was much younger than he was, probably between fifteen and seventeen years old when they were married—the average age of marriage for female colonists born in Maryland. Since Anne would have been too old and too sickly to have been the mother of the baby in the smallest lead coffin, Carr and Henry Miller think that Jane was the child's mother. Although no documents have been found to confirm a child from the second marriage, only the child of a very important person—Philip Calvert, for example—would have qualified for a lead-coffin burial.

The identification of the remains as those of Anne and Philip Calvert presented the team with another curious puzzle. Anne Wolsey Calvert died two years before Philip, yet the grave shaft stratigraphy showed they were buried at the same time, inside the same grave shaft—presumably after Philip died. Where had Anne's coffin been for the intervening two years? One scenario is that the entire grave had been dug when Anne died, wide enough for both husband and wife. In this scenario, Anne would have been placed in one side of the shaft, which was left open so that Philip's coffin could be buried beside her when he died. Miller doesn't think this is likely, though, because pollen would have sifted into the unoccupied side of the crypt. There was no pollen under Philip's coffin.

There was also no evidence that Anne's coffin had been dug up and then reburied beside Philip. Miller is sure that if this had occurred, the lead coffin would have been nicked by whatever tools were used to dig it up. The coffin had no such nicks. So Anne's coffin must have been stored somewhere. Was it awaiting shipment to England for burial there but then given a final resting place in the colony when Philip died? So far, the team hasn't discovered the answer to this riddle. Still, the shared grave of the lead-coffin family has revealed a wealth of information about the lives and deaths of St. Mary's City's most well-to-do residents.

Chapter Eight

EXPECT THE UNEXPECTED

IN 1659—EIGHT YEARS BEFORE THE PRIESTS OF ST. MARY'S CITY BUILT THE BRICK CHAPEL UNDER WHICH THE LEAD-COFFIN PEOPLE WERE EVENTUALLY BURIED—Maryland's colonial government granted a parcel of land to an Englishman named Thomas Taylor. Described in the historical record as a "gentleman," Taylor established a tobacco plantation on the site, which is located north of St. Mary's City, across the Chesapeake Bay. Although little is known of him, historians do know that over the next hundred years, the land was farmed by subsequent owners, who grew tobacco, corn, and apples. Later, during the 1900s, the property was given the name Harleigh by the people who lived there.

In 2004 Maryland archaeologist Darrin Lowery was trekking along the ridge of a low hill near a tidal creek on the Harleigh property. His eyes were caught by something peculiar: a number of large cobblestones placed about the hill's ridge. From his studies of the geology of the area, Lowery knew that the hill had been formed thousands of years earlier, when winds had swept very fine silt and sand, mounding it

COBBLESTONES CAUGHT THE eye of Darrin Lowery at what came to be known as Harleigh Knoll. They told him the site might have been a cemetery. (Archaeologists used ribbons to label the stones.)

HARLEIGH KNOLL, located across the Chesapeake Bay and north of St. Mary's City, looked like anything but a burial place. It was overgrown with trees and grasses and surrounded by a small creek.

into a knoll about 15 feet (4.6 m) high. While the wind had been strong enough to carry fine sand, it certainly couldn't have carried the cobbles that Lowery had seen. Each one looked as if it weighed a couple of pounds (0.9 kg). But Lowery was sure he'd seen similarly arranged cobbles somewhere else.

Finally, he remembered: the cobbles he'd seen had been in a colonial cemetery. They'd been used as grave markers. But the knoll wasn't near a church or any sort of building at all. It was out in the country, surrounded by trees, grasses, and the meandering tidal creek. Could this little knoll be a graveyard? Doug Owsley and his team of archaeologists, along with a group of Maryland students and teachers whom he had specially trained for the task, were called in to investigate.

For archaeological purposes, the site was given the name Harleigh Knoll. Given that the historical record showed the land had been granted to a colonist during the seventeenth century, Owsley hoped to locate graves belonging to people who had lived during that period. Still, since very little was known about the Harleigh Knoll area, he alerted his team to be on the lookout for the unexpected. As archaeologist Dana Kollmann recalled, "[Owsley] advised us that 'surprises' were a possibility."

First, "the site was gridded and mapped," said archaeologist Laurie Burgess. "Then ground-penetrating radar was used to identify potential burials." The GPR revealed that the knoll contained thirty-five underground features, spaced at regular intervals from one another, many of which were the right size for graves. Some of the underground features were located close to the cobbles that Darrin Lowery had observed. Since GPR can't create an identifiable image of a buried object, the team couldn't conclusively declare that the features were graves. Still, the GPR evidence pointed strongly in that direction.

WILLIAM HANNA (*right*) and John Imlay (*left*) drag a ground-penetrating radar (GPR) antenna across Harleigh Knoll. The echoes from the radar indicate where buried objects, such as coffins, might lie.

The First Discoveries

The landowner gave the team permission to excavate twelve of the suspected features. Each feature was assigned to an archaeologist, who directed the excavation, and a work crew. The dirt removed from the potential grave shafts was sifted through mesh screens to catch any artifacts that it might contain. Digging in the fine sand was easy, but maintaining the high standards of precision that characterize the work of Owsley and his team was not. "At archaeological sites with soil that's loamy or contains clay, it's easy to have straight, clean sidewalls [sides

WORK CREWS REMOVED DIRT (*above*) and sifted the soil (*below*) of twelve different spots on Harleigh Knoll.

of an excavated shaft]," explained Burgess. "The sandy deposits at Harleigh Knoll made straight sidewalls impossible to maintain . . . . The soil had a texture that was like fine sugar."

As the crew excavated, it became clear the soil had not lain undisturbed for several hundred years. It was crisscrossed with stains left by twisting tree roots that had grown down into the soil and then died and decomposed. Other stains showed that animals had disturbed the soil by digging burrows.

Soon several of the crews began to uncover fragile pieces of wood. The shape of the pieces, the soil stain patterns around them, and the presence of rust-covered nails told the team they had found the remains of coffins. The Harleigh Knoll site was indeed a cemetery.

Because wood decomposes fairly quickly in the Chesapeake area, it's rare to find wooden remains of colonial coffins. The knoll's fine, sandy soil was the key to the preservation in this case. Water drains through sand quickly, so the coffins buried on the knoll hadn't rested in moist soil for long periods of time.

The elated team members bagged samples of the wood for

laboratory analysis and placed brightly colored markers in the exact spots and positions of the nails to record their locations. The markers were photographed in situ to create a permanent record so the archaeologists would know how the separate parts of each coffin—the sides, the headboard, the footboard, and the lid—had been nailed together.

As excavations proceeded, archaeologist Dale Brown encountered a strange situation at a grave designated as Harleigh Knoll Burial 9 (HK9). Kari Bruwelheide had begun working at the head of the grave and Brown at the foot. They were soon confronted with a puzzle. The coffin wood Brown was exposing near the foot lay at a strange angle in relation to the long piece of wood Bruwelheide was uncovering at the other end. The pieces should have been parallel, facing the same direction. Instead, one piece was turned. The archaeologists knew that colonial coffins were not constructed in this pattern. What could the explanation be?

KARI BRUWELHEIDE (*top*) AND DALE BROWN (*bottom*) work on Burial 9. The exposed bone belongs to HK9.

Before the team could solve this mystery, Brown encountered a second oddity. As he brushed soil from the remnants of the coffin lid, he found an oyster shell in an area that would have been the top of the coffin, right in the center. It turned out to be the only shell found at Harleigh Knoll that was associated with a grave. Had it fallen atop the coffin naturally, as the grave shaft was filled in? Or had a relative or

friend placed it there to honor the deceased person's memory? We may never know the answer.

Bruwelheide did, however, find the answer to the first puzzle. The wood that she had uncovered lay at a strange angle to Brown's wood because it belonged to another coffin—a very small one. The shaft held not one coffin but two. Bruwelheide excavated the small coffin and immediately identified the bones inside it as those of a human infant. The remains, labeled as HK9A, were photographed and removed for further study in the laboratory.

THE OYSTER SHELL (*top*) found in one of the graves continues to puzzle researchers. Meanwhile, Bruwelheide brushed soil from the skull of an infant labeled HK9A (*left*). Soon the team was able to view the baby's entire skeleton (*right*).

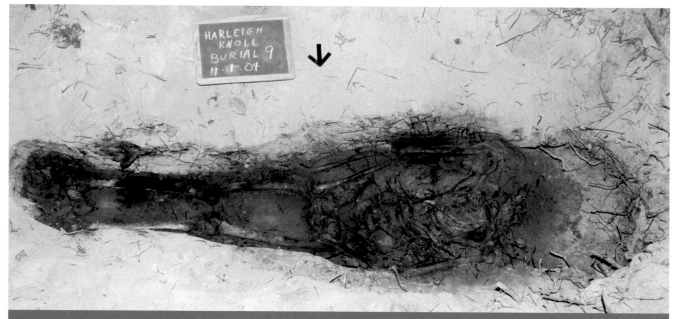

HK9 WAS MISSING THE SKULL, but the rest of the bones were in good shape. They helped researchers identify him as a man who died around age sixty in the early 1700s. Without the skull, though, they couldn't tell what his ancestry was.

The Headless Man

Meanwhile, Brown continued to excavate HK9, the other coffin in the grave shaft. The remains had been placed inside with care. The skeleton's legs and feet were straight, the arms lay alongside the body, and the hands had been positioned across the pelvis. Imagine, then, how startled Brown was when he cleared away the soil at the head end of the coffin, where he expected to find the skull. Instead, he found a third puzzle: the skull was missing! Where could it be? Had this individual been beheaded?

Careful interpretation of the coffin remnants and clues from the soil solved the mystery. The infant's coffin actually lay inside part of HK9's coffin. The only way the small coffin could have ended up within the large one was if the infant had been buried at a later time, after HK9's coffin had begun to decompose. It seems likely that the people burying the baby were unaware of the location of the previous grave. By accident, the gravediggers had disturbed the head of HK9's grave and dislodged the skull.

Brown and Bruwelheide excavated more soil from the area around the end of HK9's coffin. They found one tooth, a molar, so they knew that the skull had been there. But there was no further trace of it. The skull's whereabouts remain a mystery.

HK9's bones, while showing evidence of age, were in fairly sturdy condition. Some of the smaller bones had been decayed somewhat, and the right clavicle had been broken in two sometime after burial. Other bones had scratchlike marks on them—etchings made by roots that grew into the coffin.

The robust quality of the long bones and the pelvic bones enabled Bruwelheide to determine the skeleton had belonged to a man. That he was an adult was also apparent. The epiphyses of his long bones were completely fused. And the edges of some of his vertebrae had lipping, the bony spurs caused by arthritis. Together, these signs indicated the man had been about sixty years old or older when he died.

Hopes that the Harleigh Knoll burials would date to the seventeenth century dimmed when Brown and Bruwelheide found a brass button among the man's remains. They knew that it was unlikely that a person in the 1600s would have been buried dressed in clothes. Furthermore, the button resembled others they had seen that dated to the 1700s. More detailed study of the button would be necessary to confirm their suspicion.

Another Surprise

A skeleton designated as Harleigh Knoll Burial 7 (HK7) had been uncovered several feet away from HK9. The well-preserved coffin, whose narrow shape suggested that the remains placed inside had belonged to a person of slight stature, perfectly illustrated how a coffin breaks apart when it decays. As the wide, flat lid decomposes, it weakens until it can no longer support the weight of the soil lying on top of it. The lid collapses inward, on top of the skeleton.

That's exactly what Dana Kollmann found as she excavated HK7's coffin. In fact, the skull was still covered by large pieces of the lid.

HK7 (*above*), FOUND NEAR HK9, told a different story.

As eager as she was to see the skeleton that lay beneath, Kollmann left the wood in place on top of the skull. She continued brushing dirt from the coffin until the entire lid was exposed. "We needed to make certain that we had adequate photographs, measurements, and sketches before the coffin wood was removed," Kollmann explained.

Finally, Kollmann removed the wood and exposed the skeleton. She expected to find the remains of a person who had come from Europe, most likely England. After all, the majority of Chesapeake colonists were English. The sight of the skull, however, immediately turned that assumption upside down.

"I suspected that the person was not European once I saw the face," Kollmann recalled. "There were features of the mid-face that were consistent with an individual of African ancestry." Owsley's examination of HK7's skull confirmed Kollmann's suspicion. The angle of the front of the jaw, the rounded forehead, and the broad nasal opening were consistent with those of a person of African heritage.

THE SHAPE OF THE SKULL gave archaeologist Dana Kollmann (below, left) the clue that this person was of African ancestry.

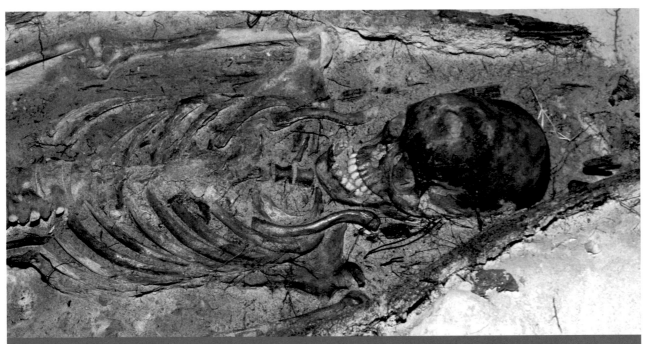

ALTHOUGH KOLLMANN HADN'T EXPECTED to find a person of African ancestry, she wasn't terribly surprised. By the late 1600s, people from Africa were working throughout the Chesapeake region.

From African Shores

Owsley and his team knew that HK7 was far from the first person of African heritage to live in the Maryland colony. According to the historical record, that distinction belongs to Mathias de Sousa, the first known documented person of African heritage to arrive in the colony of Maryland. Although he is mentioned by name in only a few documents, historians have been able to piece together some understanding of his life and standing in the colony. Thought to be the son of an African woman and a Portuguese man, de Sousa arrived in 1634 as the indentured servant—not the slave—of Father White, a Catholic priest. De Sousa became a trader and sailor. He was very active in the St. Mary's City community and eventually served in the legislative assembly. As an assembly member, he likely voted on proposed laws for the colony. This means he may have been the first person of African ancestry to vote in America.

By 1650 several hundred people of African ancestry lived in the Chesapeake area. Some were indentured servants, some were slaves, and some were free people. Regardless of their social status, the new arrivals became significant members of the colonial workforce. During most of the seventeenth century, white servants, black servants, and black slaves worked side by side on plantations, doing similar tasks. Most shared living quarters as well.

During most of this time, free black colonists had legal rights similar to those of white colonists. Court records in Virginia and Maryland prove that at least some Africans and African Americans brought grievances to the legal system and won their cases. Gradually, however, Africans and their descendants were stripped of their rights as harsh new laws concerning slavery were passed.

By 1700 slavery had become firmly established in the Chesapeake area. The thousands of Africans who were forcibly brought from Africa to the Maryland and Virginia colonies as slaves were regarded by law as property that could be bought and sold for life. When a female slave had a child, the child was considered a slave too. This meant that the supply of future workers increased with each birth. Increasingly, landowners found it more advantageous to own slaves rather than pay to bring servant workers from England. By the 1720s, slave labor had become the main workforce.

The colonial graves that Owsley's crew excavated at Harleigh Knoll contained the remains of four children, whose ancestry could not be definitely determined; six adults of African ancestry, including HK7; one person of European ancestry; and one person of unknown heritage—HK9, whose ancestry remains unknown since his skull could not be examined. At this point in the investigation, no one could determine whether the colonists buried on Harleigh Knoll were servants, slaves, or free people. Their bones can't supply the answer. Perhaps another piece of evidence would emerge as the team continued its work.

NOT ALL THE PEOPLE of African ancestry living in Maryland at this time were slaves. Mathias de Sousa, for example, arrived in the colony as an indentured servant but eventually won his freedom. He was active in life around St. Mary's City and served in its legislature. His name, listed as Matt das Sousa (*third name, left column*), on this legislative document is part of the historical record.

A Full Day's Work

Meanwhile, further information gleaned from the skull, pelvic bones, long bones, and teeth gave Owsley the information he needed to conclude that HK7 was a young woman, eighteen or nineteen years old when she died. He estimated her height at about 5 feet (1.5 m).

A green stain on the front of the cranium proved that her body had been shrouded. All of her teeth were in place and nicely spaced except for her wisdom teeth. They had never formed at all. (Some people don't develop wisdom teeth.) Only two molars showed the first traces of developing cavities. Kari Bruwelheide theorized that the condition of the young woman's teeth may have been the result of the naturally high fluoride content in the area's water supply. (Fluoride slows down the rate of tooth decay.)

As Owsley measured HK7's skeleton in situ, he looked for signs of what might have caused her death but couldn't find anything obvious. Nor did the laboratory examination reveal any signs of an ongoing disease that had persisted long enough to affect her bones. The cause of her death remains a mystery.

The laboratory examination of both HK7 and HK9 did provide evidence, however, that both

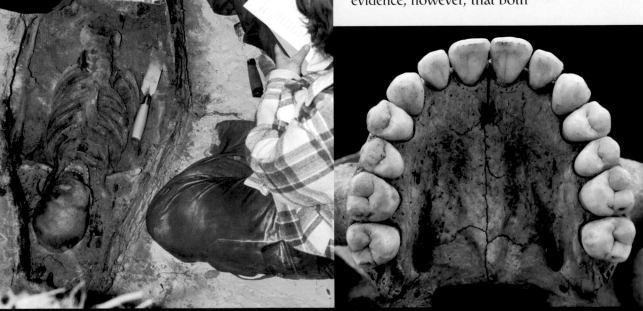

THE WORK AT HARLEIGH KNOLL continued. Measurements (*above left*) helped Doug Owsley determine that HK7 was a woman in her late teens. Her teeth (*above right*) were in very good condition.

individuals labored very hard for much of their lives. As the lead-coffin people of St. Mary's City showed, everyone who lived in seventeenth- and eighteenth-century America worked—often from dawn until dusk. Heating houses, washing clothes, hunting for meat, growing crops, and even walking or boating from one place to another—all these required labor.

HK9's humeri, or upper arm bones, had enlarged areas that proved he had used his arms for tasks that demanded strong upper arm muscles. While this bone evidence didn't specifically reveal what tasks HK9 performed, the historical record and archaeological discoveries have demonstrated that colonists routinely did several kinds of work that required significant upper body and arm strength. For example, early Maryland planters didn't have plows or other large farm implements. Land had to be cleared and prepared for planting entirely by hand. To solve this problem, the colonists copied the farming methods of Native Americans. Instead of cutting down and removing all the trees, they saved labor by removing only the small trunks, leaving larger ones still standing.

Even this minimal preparation required wielding an ax for hours on end. But that wasn't all. Next, workers had to drag away the trees they'd cut and split them into clapboards and timbers to build houses and other plantation buildings. Swinging a heavy, long-handled maul, or hammer, to pound a metal wedge into a tree trunk took plenty of muscle power. But that was the only way to split a tree trunk into rails for fences and logs for firewood.

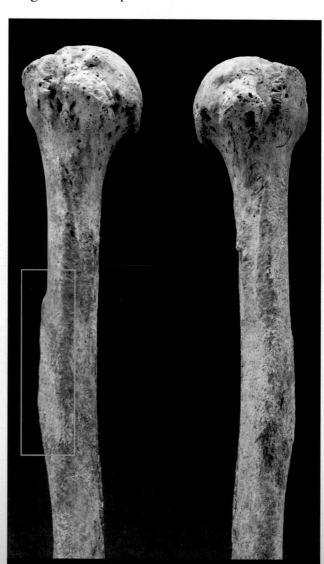

THE WORK OF SLAVES or servants at this time was mostly by hand. The researchers knew the bones would show exceptional muscle development if the buried people had been farm workers. The researchers compared the arm bones of HK9 (*above*). The bone on the left is from his right arm and shows more robust development, suggesting he used his right arm more than his left.

The labor didn't end there, either. Planting and maintaining crops took enormous effort. The historical record notes that the plantation at Harleigh Knoll produced tobacco, which would have required the majority of the time and energy of the planter's workforce. Maryland law also required planters to grow enough corn to feed the people who lived on their land—about 2 acres (0.8 hectares) per worker. Both crops were planted in small hills of soil, each about a foot (0.3 m) high, which had to be hoed by hand. If moving dirt around doesn't sound that difficult, consider this: together, the iron head and the wooden shaft of the average seventeenth-century hilling hoe weighed about 4 pounds (1.8 kg). And a single acre (0.4 hectares) of tobacco contained about twenty-seven hundred hills! (An acre of corn, whose plants needed more space, usually had about twelve hundred hills.) As the plants grew, weeds grew along with them and had to be chopped away. A different type of hoe was used for this task—and it weighed

FARM TOOLS (*above*) were simply made. The intensive labor to wield them—to cut down trees, to split the wood into logs, to plant and weed crops, and to harvest them—meant the workers' days were long and hard (*below*).

even more than a hilling hoe. When the crops were ready for harvesting, they had to be not only cut down but also bundled and carried out of the fields.

Labor of this kind, repeated over a period of years, is hard on the body. As Bruwelheide had noticed during the excavation, HK9's vertebrae displayed lipping, indicating that he suffered from spinal arthritis. This kind of arthritis is often related to wear and tear and is consistent with a lifetime of repetitive labor.

The backbone also showed signs of a condition called diffuse idiopathic skeletal hyperostosis, or DISH. DISH is more common in men than women, and it usually occurs in people over fifty years old. "DISH is found in people whose lives were characterized by strenuous physical activity," explained Owsley. Doctors are uncertain what causes it, but its effects are clear. DISH makes the tendons and ligaments along the spine harden. The bone along the sides of the vertebrae grows excessively, so much so that the vertebrae often fuse together, causing loss of mobility of the spine. The bone growth may be so severe that the bone comes to resemble a partially burned candle with hardened drops of wax along

A FARMWORKER'S BACK took continual abuse. HK9's spine (*left*) showed signs of a disease called DISH, which appears mostly in older men. Several of his vertebrae slowly fused together (*inset*), making it hard for him to move.

its length. Nine of HK9's vertebrae were fused in this manner, in three separate sections. Bruwelheide noted that even more vertebrae had been fused, but they had broken apart sometime after burial. As a person afflicted with DISH, HK9 had a stiff back. At times he experienced pain—particularly in the morning, before he'd had a chance to move and stretch his muscles.

As Bruwelheide and Owsley examined HK9's skeleton, other archaeologists tracked down information about the button found among the man's remains. Made of brass, the button was 0.6 inches (1.5 cm) wide. By comparing it with other buttons whose manufacture dates were known, the archaeologists were able to determine that HK9's button was made between 1726 and 1776. Thus he could not have died before 1726 and most likely died sometime during this fifty-year period.

Because HK7 was buried near the old man, at about the same depth and aligned in the same direction, the people who dug the second grave must have known and remembered the location and alignment of the first. HK9 and HK7, therefore, died within a few years of each other. Hence the button may shed some light on the circumstances of HK7's life. The historical record indicates that during the period in which the button had been made, the people who owned the knoll had also owned slaves. Also during that period, the majority of Africans and African Americans in Maryland were slaves. So it seems likely—though not certain—that HK7 and the other people of African heritage buried at Harleigh Knoll were slaves. And if HK9 was African as well, it is equally likely that he was a slave.

THE BUTTON FOUND among the remains of HK9 helped archaeologists date his time of death to between 1726 and 1776. Because HK9 and HK7 were buried close together, researchers thought it likely that she had also lived during that time period.

What kind of work might HK7 have been required to do as a slave? When Owsley and Bruwelheide examined her arm bones in the laboratory, they noticed muscle attachment sites that indicated she frequently flexed and extended her elbows. During the mid-eighteenth century in Maryland, the majority of enslaved women worked in the fields, just like the men. Thus HK7 probably hoed tobacco, inspected the leaves of the growing plants for pests such as hornworms and cutworms, and removed poor-quality leaves near the base of the plant to allow the upper leaves to grow larger.

If she hadn't worked in the fields, grinding corn may have been one of her chores. After corn was harvested, dried, and removed from the cob, it had to be ground into meal so that it could be used to make bread and mush. Unless there was a nearby mill where the planter could take the dried kernels to be ground by machine, this step had to be done by hand with a mortar and pestle. This tiring task topped the list of household drudgery. It required raising and dropping an iron pestle—which weighed as much as 5 pounds (2.3 kg)—many thousands of times to crush the corn into miniscule pieces.

Preparing wool to make cloth also requires flexing and extending the elbows. During the 1600s, all cloth in

ARCHAEOLOGISTS WERE JUST AS INTERESTED in the life of HK7. Her arm bones told them she worked both arms a great deal. If she worked close to the house, she might have used a mortar and pestle to grind corn (*above*) or she might have combed wool fibers to clean and straighten them for spinning into yarn (*facing page*), as demonstrated by these reenactors.

the Chesapeake colonies was imported from Europe, but by the mid-1700s, some planters in the region had begun producing cloth. If the planter who owned the knoll property had been among them, HK7's work might have included a process called carding. A clump of wool is placed on a paddle with rows of narrowly spaced wire teeth on it. A second, similarly toothed paddle is pressed into the wool and pulled through it. The teeth of the two paddles align the wool fibers so that they can be spun together into yarn on a spinning wheel. These actions must be

repeated several times for each clump of wool.

Any of these jobs, along with less complex ones such as hauling buckets of water from a well and doing laundry, would have caused HK7 to develop strong arm muscles. While her bones clearly indicate that she used her arms for strenuous physical activity, it's impossible to conclude exactly which tasks she did—only that they were numerous and that she'd done them since she was a little girl.

To add to this slowly growing portrait of the lives of the Harleigh Knoll people, the team sent samples from the remains for carbon-13 analysis. HK9, the old man, had a carbon-13 value of –13.8. HK7's carbon value was –11.1. Both values are consistent with those of a person who has eaten a corn-based diet for a long period of time. (Remember, an English carbon-13 value is –21 to –18.)

No one knows if either HK7 or HK9 was born in Maryland. The question of their birthplaces joins several other unknowns about the people of Harleigh Knoll. We can't be certain whether HK7 and HK9 were slaves, indentured servants, or free persons—or exactly what types of work they did. We may never learn how they died, whether they were related, or even if they knew each other. But we do know that they were well regarded by family or friends. Unlike the boy at Leavy Neck, both were buried with care and respect when their lives of intense labor ended.

Chapter Nine

REMEMBER ME

THE SCIENTISTS AND HISTORIANS who have studied the human remains found throughout the colonial Chesapeake area have learned a great deal about these individuals. From their diet and health to their social status, many secrets once lost to time have become part of our recorded history again. One thing that no one could determine in a laboratory or an archive, however, was what the colonists had looked like when they were alive. Very few were drawn or painted in their lifetimes. Written descriptions of any but the most famous are rare.

Forensic artists focus on solving the puzzle of appearance. Working with forensic anthropologists, these skilled specialists use skull analyses to create lifelike images of the dead. The key to this endeavor is the fact that many facial features of a living person are determined by bone features of the person's skull. Someone with a wide face has broad cheekbones, for example, while a bent, beaklike nose corresponds with a similarly shaped nasal bridge, the bone above the nasal hole.

The first step in creating a facial reconstruction is to make an exact replica of the skull to eliminate any risk of damaging the original. Replicas can be made in several ways. For example, the skull of the teenage girl from Harleigh Knoll was reproduced with a computerized tomography scan, or CT scan. This type of scan is used in the medical field to create images of tumors and other internal medical conditions. Instead of making a single image, as a regular X-ray machine would, a CT scanner makes many digital images, called slices, which form a complete image when combined. Each slice contains hundreds of digital measurements. A computer translates these measurements into points that can be plotted on a three-dimensional (3-D) grid. When all the points are plotted, a 3-D image of the skull can be displayed on a computer's monitor.

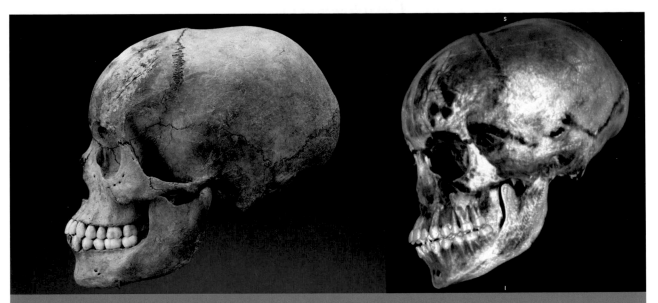

TO CREATE THE REPLICA SKULL, HK7's real skull *(left)* was scanned by a **CT** scanner. The computer created a virtual image of the skull *(right)* that was used to make the replica skull.

The image created by a CT scan is digital. It exists only within the computer. For the artist to create a facial reconstruction, the image must be translated into a solid object. A technician transfers the digital data to sophisticated machinery that uses computer-guided precision tools to manufacture a replica skull. The result accurately reflects the surface features of the original skull—including the tiniest cracks, depressions, and raised areas.

Joanna Hughes, the forensic artist who created a clay reconstruction of HK7's face, began her work by placing an artificial eye in each of the replica skull's eye sockets. Noting HK7's African ancestry, Hughes selected brown eyes. Next, she consulted a chart created by anthropologists based on known measurements of facial tissue and the underlying muscles. Using this data as a guide, Hughes glued markers to the replica to represent the thickness of the living tissue and muscles a person of HK7's age, size,

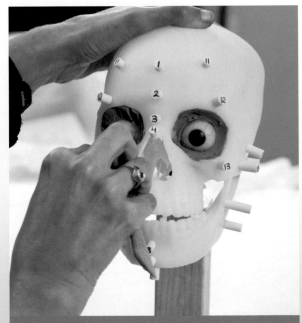

FORENSIC ARTIST JOANNA HUGHES placed markers on the replica skull to stand for the thickness of skin and facial muscles.

and ancestry would have most likely possessed. "I use about fifteen markers per skull. The markers are actually erasers. They're placed on specific points on the skull," explained Hughes.

Based on the size and location of the markers, Hughes added oil-based clay to the replica to form tissue and features. Oil-based clay doesn't dry. It remains soft to the touch, so the artist can rework the features as needed. "The hardest features to do are the ears and the eyelids," Hughes noted. "Ears are very complex because there are lots of nooks and crannies that are hard to sculpt. And eyelids are very small and thin."

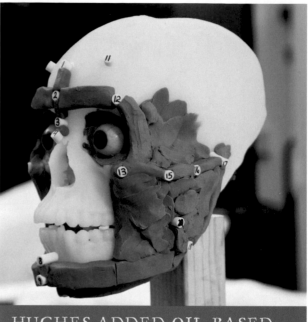

HUGHES ADDED OIL-BASED clay to flesh out the features.

Owsley and Bruwelheide worked closely with Hughes as she developed the reconstruction. They made suggestions and corrections based on their analyses of the skull's shape and features. Once her work was complete, the soft clay reconstruction was shipped to StudioEIS, a sculpture and design studio whose sculptors specialize in creating historically accurate sculpture. "We continue the process from where [the forensic artists] left off, using exactly what they've given us, but in a different, permanent material," explained Ivan Schwartz, the studio's founder and director.

The sculptors began by creating a plaster mold of Hughes's clay sculpture. "The wet plaster is applied directly to the oil-based clay [and allowed to solidify]," explained Schwartz. Because oil-based clay repels the water in plaster, the hardened plaster didn't stick to the clay. The resulting plaster mold was pulled off the sculpture and filled with water-based clay. StudioEIS sculptors then removed this clay cast from the mold and began to finalize the details of the reconstruction.

The sculptors added precise features to give the reconstruction the look of a living person. By adding clay in one area and removing it from another, by looking at a living teenage girl whose bone structure resembled that of HK7, by noting the small details of individual faces—the curve of the tip of an ear or the way skin lies over a cheek or jaw—and by keeping in mind the structural reflections Hughes had created, the sculptors meticulously added lifelike characteristics around the girl's eyes, mouth, and chin.

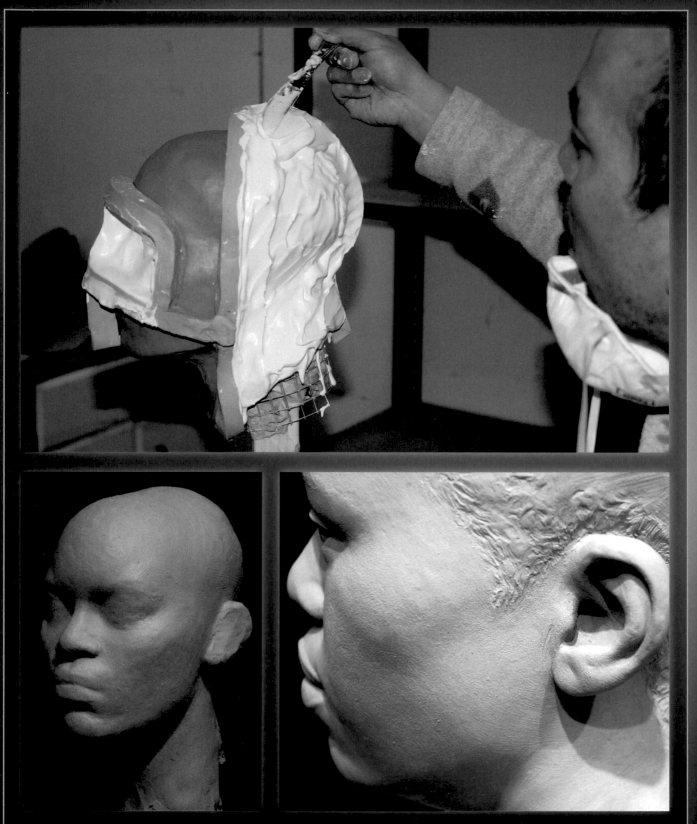

HUGHES'S CLAY-COVERED RECONSTRUCTION WAS SENT to StudioEIS, a
sculpture and design studio that specializes in historically accurate sculptures. There the first step was to create
a plaster mold (*top*) of Hughes's model. The mold was filled with water-based clay to provide a pliable model that
the artists could sculpt further (*above left*). They added details such as ears and eyelids and hair (*above right*).

The use of clay allowed the sculptors to continually refine these details until Owsley and Bruwelheide gave their approval to create the final, permanent reconstruction. The sculptors then created one more mold by applying a flexible, rubbery material called silicone to the sculpture, allowing it to dry, and peeling it off the clay. The silicone mold was filled with plaster. After this plaster cast dried, an artist painted it to complete the facial reconstruction. The result is a lasting, durable sculpture worthy of museum display. It's also the first such reconstruction of an American colonist of African ancestry.

The creation of facial reconstructions perfectly illustrates how two seemingly different disciplines—science and art—can complement each other. The combination of Owsley and Bruwelheide's scientific analysis and interpretation of a skull's bony features with the artistic talents of sculptors who specialize in forensic work gives us a rare opportunity. Despite the passage of centuries, we can come face-to-face with people who lived long ago, further strengthening the skeletal story that has already established a connection between us.

THE RESULT OF THESE EFFORTS is a lifelike reconstruction of HK7—the first of a colonist of African ancestry.

A Feeling That Moves You

As more men and women streamed to the Chesapeake region from England and elsewhere, new cities were founded. Just as Jamestown was eventually replaced by a new capital in a better location for trade, St. Mary's City gave way to Annapolis. Slowly, people moved away. The city's buildings fell into disrepair. Their wood and stone were hauled away and used to construct new dwellings and shops and churches in other towns. As time passed, soil covered the old foundations, and farmers planted their crops in the soil. St. Mary's City, like Jamestown, was forgotten—but not forever.

Over the past fifty years, archaeologists and forensic anthropologists have studied the graves of more than three hundred seventeenth-century Chesapeake colonists from many different sites in Virginia and Maryland. Their work is not finished. "New technologies are being developed all the time. Today's young people will be the new generation of scientists who will examine colonial remains using better technologies than we have today. They will be the ones who answer the questions that we can't answer now," Owsley stated. Meanwhile, recently discovered buildings and graves at James Fort, St. Mary's City, and other colonial sites continue to provide information about America's past.

ARCHAEOLOGISTS MEASURE and document the findings of two more graves inside St. Mary's brick chapel. The second grave lies directly beneath the first. Only the feet of the second burial are visible.

No matter how many graves scientists excavate, there will always be more information to discover about the Chesapeake's first European and African settlers. "Studying one or two skeletons can provide information about a single individual—who they were physically and what they may have experienced," Kari Bruwelheide observed. "But studying many skeletons provides information about an entire group of people—a population—their mortality [death] patterns, health, general activity patterns and even cultural practices."

Bruwelheide has found inspiration in the chance to enhance the historical record with the discovery of physical evidence too. "Skeletal remains provide us with the additional opportunity to document or confirm the historical record in a tangible way—for example, the struggle at Jamestown during the Starving Time, or an attack on James Fort, as evidenced in the remains of JR1225B, the boy with the arrowhead in his leg."

The archaeological excavation of seventeenth- and eighteenth-century graves also gives us a new perspective on colonial customs. As Henry Miller noted, "The entire subject of how seventeenth-century Chesapeake colonists treated their dead is not recorded in the historical record. As a result of excavating the graves, we have new information about burial rituals, whether they used a shroud or a coffin, how the coffins were constructed, and the amount of care taken to bury a loved one."

Such studies have helped scholars to better understand how traditions and customs from many places in England were maintained or blended together in America. "There is a surprising diversity of coffin types used at St. Mary's City, some not seen before in America," Miller observed. "We think this is because the Chesapeake colonists (unlike New England colonists) came from a variety of areas in England, and each area had distinctive ways of living. This is a powerful clue to enduring cultural connections that are often not expressed in written evidence."

The field of medicine is enriched by forensic anthropology as well. Colonial remains provide insight into causes of death and illness. For example, the colonists' teeth showed a much higher rate of decay after they began eating a corn-based diet compared to before. "Corn is high in carbohydrates, substances that contain sugar," Owsley explained. "It's also sticky, so it clings to the teeth. When corn became a main ingredient in the colonial diet, people got more cavities, which led to abscesses, which led to tooth loss."

Forensic studies also show how the bones of populations of people respond to physical labor, disease, and harsh living conditions—all of which the Chesapeake

THE BRICK CHAPEL in St. Mary's City where the lead-coffin people were found is being completely reconstructed. It will give people yet another way to experience the past.

settlers knew well. The discovery that many Chesapeake colonial children suffered from rickets surprised Owsley. Historians already knew that rickets were common in England during the last half of the 1800s, when the Industrial Revolution led to the widespread building of factories. In those days, factories pumped large amounts of coal pollution into the air, reducing the amount of sunlight that reached people's skin. The lack of sunlight, which provides vitamin D, caused a large number of English children to develop rickets.

In contrast, the air in the Chesapeake during colonial times was unpolluted by manufacturing wastes. Rickets seemed oddly out of place. "But when you take the cultural custom of swaddling into account, that explains it," Owsley observed. "The tightly wrapped infants didn't receive adequate amounts of sunlight or vitamin D." As more information from colonial skeletons is gathered and examined, Owsley expects that additional discoveries about health and medicine will be made.

As useful and fascinating as these discoveries are, the gathering of data is not the only goal that motivates these scientists. In the words of Carter Hudgins, "Excavating and researching recovered artifacts is one thing, but to come face to face with a person always has an impact. Not a scary feeling. It's a feeling that moves you. At Jamestown, for example, suddenly we can associate the place with the people and the hardships they faced. It puts our work into a larger perspective."

This sense of meaning—the ability to find a new connection to the past—is a recurring theme for many who have devoted their careers to archaeology and forensic anthropology. "We can shed some light on who these people were and how they lived and died," Bruwelheide observed. "This information lets us view history in terms we can intimately understand—at the human and individual level. In knowing better the story of these first immigrants, we might better understand how we got to where we are as a nation."

Miller described his work as a sort of tribute to the people whose remains he studies. "The fact that we can learn from these colonists and gain a deeper understanding of them and their times is a way of giving them respect. Although their names are usually lost to time, we can still recognize their existence and honor their lives," he concluded. Owsley added, "Most of these people lived their whole lives without anyone writing a word about them. The information we gather from their skeletons is, in essence, their legacy."

Each time an archaeologist excavates a grave, we are given the opportunity to come face-to-face with a person who was once someone's son or daughter. And as each skeleton reveals its secrets, history takes on new life. The bones of the Chesapeake colonists prove that they endured pain or endless toil or frequent illness. Some lived well, and some did not. Some were buried well, and some were not.

From the basement grave at Leavy Neck to the Captain's honorable resting place with his leading staff, from the simple but respectful wooden coffins of Harleigh Knoll to the luxurious lead coffins of St. Mary's City, the graves and the remains of colonial settlers carry a message to the people of today. They remind us not to forget their lives and accomplishments—and not to lose our connection to the past. A broken tooth, a fractured bone, an arthritic back, and strands of brown hair—all of them whisper: *"Rest with me for a moment or two. I have a story to tell."* These tales, written only in bone, await those with the patience to find them.

FINIS

Source Notes

9   Douglas Owsley, personal communication to author, September 10, 2005.

18   Carter C. Hudgins, e-mail to author, August 2, 2006.

20–21   William Kelso, interview by author, Jamestown, VA, August 16, 2005.

21   Hudgins, telephone conversation with author, October 20, 2005.

22   Hudgins, e-mail to author, October 24, 2005.

23   Hudgins, telephone conversation, October 20, 2005.

23–24   Ibid.

25   Ibid.

27   Ibid.

35   Owsley, telephone conversation with author, October 6, 2005.

37   Michael Lavin, e-mail to author, January 25, 2006.

42   Kari Bruwelheide, e-mail to author, July 11, 2007.

42   Ibid.

43   Catherine Correll Walls, APVA/Preservation Virginia, *The Jamestown Biographies Project 2007*, Entry #789, 940, communicated to author via e-mail, July 17, 2007.

45   Kelso, interview by author, Jamestown, VA, August 15, 2005.

46   Ibid.

46   Ibid.

47   Ibid.

48   Owsley, telephone conversation with author, October 6, 2005.

50   George Percy, *Observations Gathered out of "A Discourse of the Plantation of the Southern Colony in Virginia by the English, 1606,"* ed. David B. Quinn (Charlottesville: University of Virginia Press, 1967), 24–25.

52   Kelso, interview, August 15, 2005.

53   Ibid.

53   Ibid.

55   Al Luckenbach, telephone conversation with author, October 24, 2005.

55   Ibid.

56   Ibid.

57   Ibid.

58   Ibid.

59   Ibid.

59   Ibid.

60–61   Owsley, telephone conversation with author, October 6, 2005.

62   Owsley, telephone conversation with author, June 16, 2008.

62   Owsley, telephone conversation with author, January 6, 2006.

66   Owsley. telephone conversation with author, June 3, 2008.

66–67   Owsley, telephone conversation, June 16, 2008.

68   Henry Miller, interview by author, St. Mary's City, MD, August 10, 2005.

70   Ibid.

70   Stephanie Bandy Nutt, telephone conversation with author, September 19, 2005.

70   Miller, e-mail to author, September 7, 2005.

70   Nutt, telephone conversation.

72   Ibid.

74   Tim Riordan, e-mail to author, September 19, 2005.

74   Nutt, telephone conversation.

75   Miller, interview.

79   Ibid.

85   Silas Hurry, interview by author, St. Mary's City, MD, August 10, 2005.

87   Ibid.

94   Miller, e-mail to author, January 11, 2008.

94   Owsley, telephone conversation with author, October 6, 2005.

98   Miller, interview.

100   Miller, e-mail to author, February 1, 2006.

100   Miller, interview.

101   Ibid.

102   Ibid.

106   Ibid.

110   Dana Kollmann, e-mail to author, September 5, 2006.

110   Laurie Burgess, e-mail to author, February 6, 2006.

110–111   Ibid.

116   Kollmann, e-mail.

116   Ibid.

122   Owsley, telephone conversation with author, June 26, 2008.

128   Joanna Hughes, e-mail to author, December 11, 2007.

128   Ibid.

128   Ivan Schwartz, telephone conversation with author, December 10, 2007.

128   Schwartz, e-mail to author, January 16, 2008.

131   Owsley, telephone conversation, June 28, 2008.

132   Bruwelheide, e-mail to author, January 17, 2008.

132   Ibid.

132   Miller, e-mail to author, January 11, 2008.

132   Ibid.

132   Owsley, telephone conversation with author, June 28, 2008.

133   Ibid.

133–134   Hudgins, e-mail to author, January 16, 2008.

134   Bruwelheide, e-mail to author, January 17, 2008.

134   Miller, e-mail to author, January 11, 2008.

134   Owsley, telephone conversation, June 28, 2008.

1602	Bartholomew Gosnold explores the shores of what later became Massachusetts and Maine.
1606	Three ships leave England en route to North America to found the Virginia Colony. Gosnold captains one of the ships.
1607	The ships arrive, and the all-male crew members build James Fort.
1608	The original James Fort burns to the ground. The colonists build a second fort. Ships from England carrying women colonists arrive.
1609	Spanish ambassador Pedro de Zuñiga draws a simple map of James Fort and sends it to the king of Spain.
1609–1610	A harsh winter at James Fort, during which many die, comes to be known as the Starving Time.
1619	The first Africans arrive in Jamestown.
1630s	James Fort disappears from the historical record. Cecil Calvert, Lord Baltimore, receives a land grant from King Charles I of England to found a colony in North America. Calvert names the colony Maryland after the king's wife.
1634	Ships belonging to Lord Baltimore land in North America. The colonists on board found St. Mary's City, Maryland. Mathias de Sousa, an indentured servant of African and Portuguese ancestry, arrives in Maryland.
1645–1655	During unrest in England, Lord Baltimore loses control of Maryland.
1657–1659	Lord Baltimore regains control of Maryland. Meanwhile, his half brother Philip holds various offices in Maryland.
	Colonial officials grant land in Maryland to Thomas Taylor.
1661–1675	Lord Baltimore's eldest son, Charles, is governor of Maryland.
1662-1677	William Neale acquires a property called Leavy Neck in Maryland. He lives there until his death.
1667	Catholic priests in Maryland build a chapel in St. Mary's City.
1668–1671	Philip Calvert is mayor of St. Mary's City.
1675	Cecil Calvert dies in England.

1682–1683	Philip Calvert dies in Maryland.
1693	Sir Lionel and Anne Copley die and are buried in St. Mary's City.
1700	Most people of African ancestry in the Chesapeake area are slaves.
1799	Medical students open the Copley coffins.
1852	An early photograph shows the crumbling tower of a church in Jamestown.
1890s	The Association for the Preservation of Virginia Antiquities is founded. The group protects the church ruins on the site of Jamestown.
1940s–1950s	The National Park Service excavates portions of Jamestown.
1990	Archaeologists find three lead coffins in the brick chapel at St. Mary's City. Speculation is they hold the remains of Philip Calvert; his first wife, Anne; and his infant daughter by his second wife, Jane.
1994	The Jamestown Rediscovery Project breaks ground for a new set of excavations to find James Fort.
2002	The remains of "the Captain" are found just outside James Fort's walls. Speculation is he was Bartholomew Gosnold, captain of the *Godspeed*.
2003	The Lost Towns Project finds the remains of a teenage boy on the Leavy Neck property in Maryland. Lacking a name, he comes to be called Leavy Neck boy.
2004	Archaeologist Darrin Lowery finds a cemetery on Thomas Taylor's land, called Harleigh Knoll. Eventually, twelve graves are excavated, including HK9 and HK7.
2005	Another teenage boy's remains—named JR1225B—are found inside what was the original James Fort. Speculation is he died in 1607.
2007	Forensic artists reconstruct the head and face of HK7.
2009	The Written in Bone exhibit opens at the Smithsonian Institution in Washington, D.C.

Selected Bibliography

BOOKS

Barbour, Philip L., ed. *The Complete Works of Captain John Smith (1580–1631) in Three Volumes.* Chapel Hill: University of North Carolina Press, 1986.

Bass, William M. *Human Osteology: A Laboratory and Field Manual of the Human Skeleton (Special Publication).* Springfield: Missouri Archaeological Society, 1971.

Berlin, Ira, and Philip D. Morgan, eds. *Cultivation and Culture: Labor and the Shaping of Slave Life in the Americas.* Charlottesville: University of Virginia Press, 1993.

Carr, Lois Green, Russell R. Menard, and Lorena S. Walsh. *Robert Cole's World.* Chapel Hill: University of North Carolina Press, 1991.

Carr, Lois Green, Philip D. Morgan, and Jean B. Russo. *Colonial Chesapeake Society.* Chapel Hill: University of North Carolina Press, 1998.

Clark, Alice. *Working Life of Women in the Seventeenth Century.* New York: Harcourt, 1920.

Hurry, Silas D. *"… Once the Metropolis of Maryland": The History and Archaeology of Maryland's First Capital.* St. Mary's City, MD: Historic St. Mary's City Commission, 2001.

Kelso, William M. *Jamestown Rediscovery 1994–2004.* Richmond: Association for the Preservation of Virginia Antiquities, 2004.

——. *Jamestown: The Buried Truth.* Charlottesville: University of Virginia Press, 2006.

Litten, Julian. *The English Way of Death: The Common Funeral since 1450.* London: Robert Hale, 1992.

Mays, Simon. *The Archaeology of Human Bones.* London: Routledge, 1998.

Morgan, Philip D. *Slave Counterpoint: Black Culture in the Eighteenth Century Chesapeake and Low Country.* Chapel Hill: University of North Carolina Press, 1998.

Percy, George. *Observations Gathered out of "A Discourse of the Plantation of the Southern Colony in Virginia by the English, 1606."* Edited by David B. Quinn. Charlottesville: University of Virginia Press, 1967.

Riordan, Timothy B. *Dig a Grave, Both Wide and Deep.* St. Mary's City Archaeology Series, 3. St. Mary's City, MD: Historic St. Mary's City Commission, November 2000.

Rountree, Helen C. *Pocahontas, Powhatan, Opechancanough: Three Indian Lives Changed by Jamestown.* Charlottesville: University of Virginia Press, 2005.

Scheuer, Louise, and Sue Black. Illustrated by Angela Christie. *Developmental Juvenile Osteology.* San Diego: Academic Press, 2000.

Tate, Thad W., and David Ammerman, eds. *The Chesapeake in the Seventeenth Century.* Chapel Hill: University of North Carolina Press, 1979.

Thornton, John. *Africa and Africans in the Making of the Atlantic World, 1400–1800.* New York: Cambridge University Press, 1998.

Ubelaker, Douglas H. *Human Skeletal Remains.* 3rd ed. Washington, DC: Taraxacum, 1999.

Yonge, Samuel H. *The Site of Old "James Towne," 1607–1698.* Richmond: Association for the Preservation of Virginia Antiquities, 1904.

ARTICLES

Berlin, Ira. "African Immigration to Colonial America." *History Now*, no. 3. March 2005. http://www.historynow.org/03_2005/historian3.html (August 29, 2008).

Blanton, Dennis B. "Drought as a Factor in the Jamestown Colony, 1607–1612." *Historical Archaeology* 34, no. 4 (2000): 74–81.

Bruwelheide, K., and Owsley, D. "Written in Bone: Reading the Remains of the 17th Century." *AnthroNotes* 28, no. 1 (Spring 2007): 8–14.

Carr, Lois Green, and Lorena S. Walsh. "The Planter's Wife: The Experience of White Women in Seventeenth-Century Maryland." *William and Mary Quarterly*, 3rd series, 34, no. 4 (October 1977): 542–571.

Cox, C. Jane. "Excavations at Leavy Neck, Providence Maryland: A Solitary, Poor, Nasty, Brutish and Short Life." (Draft Report. Manuscript on file with Anne Arundel County's Lost Towns Project, Anne Arundel County Planning and Zoning Department, Annapolis MD, January 2008).

Miller, Henry, Silas D. Hurry, and Timothy B. Riordan. "The Lead Coffins of St. Mary's City: An Exploration of Life and Death in Early Maryland." *Maryland Historical Magazine* 99, no. 3 (Fall 2004): 350–373.

Neely, Paula. "Tooth Test Suggest Other Identities for Jamestown Mystery Captain." *APVA.* November 20, 2006. http://APVA.org/pressroom (November 2007).

Riordan, Timothy B. "Philip Calvert: Patron of St. Mary's City." *Maryland Historical Magazine* 99, no. 3 (Fall 2004): 329–349.

Ubelaker, Douglas H., and Douglas W. Owsley. "Isotopic Evidence for Diet in the Seventeenth-Century Colonial Chesapeake." *American Antiquity* 68, no. 1 (2003): 129–139.

INTERVIEWS

Bandy Nutt, Stephanie. Phone communication, September 19, 2005; e-mails, various dates, 2007–2008.

Bruwelheide, Kari. Personal communications, e-mails, and phone calls, September 2004–2008.

Carr, Lois. Personal communication, August 2005.

Hudgins, Carter C. Personal communication, August 2005; phone, October 20, 2005; e-mails, various dates, 2005–2008.

Hughes, Joanna. E-mails, various dates, 2007.

Hurry, Silas. Personal communication, August 2005.

Karas, Vicky. E-mails, various dates, 2007–2008.

Kelso, William. Personal communication, August 2005.

Lavin, Michael. E-mails, various dates, 2006–2008.

Long, Sharon. Phone communication, September 7, 2005.

Luckenbach, Al. Phone communication, October 24, 2005; e-mails, various dates, 2006–2008.

Miller, Henry. Personal communication, e-mails, August 2005–2008.

Owsley, Douglas. Personal communications, e-mails, and phone calls, September 2004–2008.

Riordan, Tim. Personal communication, e-mails, August 2005–2006.

Further Reading and Websites

About the Powhatan Chiefdom
http://powhatan.wm.edu/
This website describes the excavation of Werowocomoco, the main village of the Powhatan chiefdom.

Carbone, Elisa. *Blood on the River: James Town 1607*. New York: Viking, 2006.
In this work of fiction, young orphan Sam Collier joins Captain John Smith as they sail to the Virginia colony and work to survive the first winter at Jamestown.

Cooper, Michael L. *Jamestown, 1607*. New York: Holiday House, 2007.

Day, Nancy. *Your Travel Guide to Colonial America*. Minneapolis: Twenty-First Century Books, 2001.

Fridell, Ron. *Forensic Science*. Minneapolis: Lerner Publications Company, 2007.

Friedlander, Mark P., Jr., and Terry M. Phillips. *When Objects Talk: Solving a Crime with Science*. Minneapolis: Twenty-First Century Books, 2001.

Gray, Edward G. *Colonial America: A History in Documents*. New York: Oxford University Press, 2003.

Historic St. Mary's
http://www.stmaryscity.org/
This website offers a wealth of information on the history and archaeology of St. Mary's City.

Jamestown Rediscovery
http://www.apva.org/jr.html
The website of the Jamestown Rediscovery Project allows visitors to find out about current digs and to get historical information about the founding and inhabitants of Jamestown.

Miller, Brandon Marie. *Growing Up in a New World 1607 to 1775*. Minneapolis: Lerner Publications Company, 2003.

Seeing Jamestown and Werowocomoco
http://magma.nationalgeographic.com/ngm/jamestown/
This interactive website has flyovers of Jamestown and the nearby Powhatan village of Werowocomoco, plus photos, games, and expert commentary.

Walker, Sally M. *Life in an Estuary*. Minneapolis: Twenty-First Century Books, 2003.

Written in Bone
http://writteninbone.si.edu
This website goes with the exhibit of the same name at the Smithsonian Institution that opens in 2009. It includes an interactive site on the Leavy Neck boy.

AUTHOR'S ACKNOWLEDGMENTS

THIS BOOK WOULD NOT HAVE BEEN POSSIBLE without the help of many scientists and historians. In Jamestown I watched Dr. Carter Hudgins excavate JR1225B's skeleton. Dr. William Kelso told me about the Rediscovery Project and showed me the Captain's skeleton. Catherine Correll Walls and Michael D. Lavin described archival searches and conservation.

At St. Mary's City, Dr. Henry Miller brought me into the brick chapel—under reconstruction at the time—so I could see where the lead-coffin people had been buried. In the laboratory, I touched the smooth surface of the lid of Philip Calvert's wooden coffin. Dr. Tim Riordan explained shrouding and shared stories about graves found in the chapel field. Silas Hurry showed me the lead-coffin lady's silk bow and hauled out the soil peel so I could peek at the grave-shaft stratigraphy. Stephanie Bandy Nutt shared the thrill of the initial discovery.

Also in Maryland, Dr. Lois Green Carr described her archival search for Philip and Anne Calvert and shared her knowledge of colonial planters. Dr. Al Luckenbach and C. Jane Cox of the Lost Towns Project communicated many details on the Leavy Neck boy and his gravesite.

Via e-mail and phone conversations, Sharon Long, Joanna Hughes, and Ivan Schwartz talked me through the artistic processes used to create a facial reconstruction. The sections on isotopes owe their clarity to Dr. Joan Brenner Coltrain. My dentist, Dr. Timothy Duez, and hygienist Kathy Banta brought me up to date on dental issues.

Excavating graves with Doug Owsley's team at Harleigh Knoll was one of the most rewarding experiences of my life. Thanks to John Akridge III for granting us permission to explore this remarkable site. I often sat on the lovely, quiet knoll and imagined what the people whose remains we were uncovering had been like while alive. I want to thank Kari Bruwelheide, Laurie Burgess, Dr. Dana Kollmann, John Imlay, and Dale Brown for putting up with my rusty archaeological skills and Dr. William Hanna for showing me the GPR equipment.

At the Smithsonian, I truly became acquainted with the colonial people featured in this book. I have held the remains of JR1225B, HK7, HK9, the Leavy Neck boy, and Anne Wolsey Calvert and examined in great detail how their bones reflect their lives and deaths. Smithsonian thanks go to Basiliki Vicky

Karas, Melvin Wachowiak, and Chris Hollshwander, who told me about crafting skull reproductions. Dr. Douglas Ubelaker answered questions during my initial research. Vicki Simon and Aleithea Williams ferreted out additional information as Cass Taylor helped me sort through hundreds of photos. Photographers Chip Clark and Brittney Tatchell provided many stunning photographs that allow readers to establish their own connections with the colonial people featured in this book.

Everyone generously shared time and knowledge as I asked "just one more question," again and again. Each of you has enriched my life and deepened my understanding of the innumerable hardships faced by all peoples—not just English men—who lived during the colonial Chesapeake period. An extra dollop of thanks goes to Dale, Henry, Carter, Al, and Kari for manuscript critiques. Last and *definitely* not least, my heartfelt thanks go to Douglas Owsley, who changed the course of my life when he asked, "Do you have time for a cup of coffee? I have an idea for a children's book." Writing this book was truly an adventure!

Index

About the Author

Sally M. Walker has brought science to life in more than fifty books for young readers. Her meticulous research and stirring storytelling in *Secrets of a Civil War Submarine: Solving the Mysteries of the H. L. Hunley* won her the prestigious Robert F. Sibert Informational Book Award Medal in 2006. She also won acclaim for *Fossil Fish Found Alive*, an ALA Notable title. In *Written in Bone*, she brings that same skill and scholarship to uncover the stories of people from the colonial era. She worked alongside scientists, forensic anthropologists, and archivists as they excavated and studied skeletons, burial practices, and remnants found in Virginia and Maryland. Ms. Walker lives in De Kalb, Illinois.

Photo Acknowledgments

Images in this book are used with permission of: National Museum of Natural History, Smithsonian Institution in Washington, D.C./courtesy of Doug Owsley, photos by Chip Clark, pp. 1 (both), 4, 5, 6, 8, (both), 15, 22 (top), 31 (top), 36 (top), 39 (both), 44 (top), 47, 48, 49, 54 (top), 55, 56, 57 (bottom), 60 (both), 61 (left), 65 (right), 66, 68, 73 (top), 74, 75, 77, 79 (bottom), 80, 82 (both), 83, 84 (all), 85, 86 (top), 88, 92, 93 (all), 94, 95 (both), 97 (left, top right), 98, 99 (both), 100, 101, 102, 103 (both), 108 (both), 109, 111 (both), 112, 113 (bottom left, bottom right), 114, 116, 117, 119 (left), 121 (both), 124, 126, 131, 133, 137 (top, third from top, fourth from top), 141; National Museum of Natural History, Smithsonian Institution in Washington, D.C./courtesy of Doug Owsley, photos by Brittney Tatchell, pp. 3, 28, 31 (bottom right), 61 (right), 62, 63, 64, 65 (left center, bottom left), 86 (bottom), 87, 89, 90, 91 (both), 96, 97 (bottom right), 113 (top), 119 (right), 120, 122 (both), 123, 127 (top left); © Laura Westlund/Independent Picture Service, pp. 10, 23, 29, 33, 41; Courtesy of APVA Preservation Virginia, pp. 11, 14 (both), 16 (both), 37, 42, 46 (both), 136 (second from top); Courtesy of APVA Preservation Virginia, photos by Michael Lavin, pp. 13, 17 (bottom), 20, 44 (bottom), 45, 52, 137 (second from top); © iStockphoto.com/Lisa Williams, p. 17 (top); Courtesy of APVA Preservation Virginia, diagram by Jamie E. May, p. 19; © Ralph Hutchings/Visuals Unlimited, Inc., p. 22 (bottom); National Museum of Natural History, Smithsonian Institution in Washington, D.C./courtesy of Doug Owsley, photos by Ken Rahaim, pp. 24, 25, 26, 27, 34, 36 (bottom), 38; National Museum of Natural History, Smithsonian Institution in Washington, D.C./courtesy of Doug Owsley, image by Kari Bruwelheide, p. 30; © Nigel Corrie/English Heritage Photographic Studio, p. 31 (bottom left); © Mansell/Time Life Pictures/Getty Images, pp. 51, 136 (top); Historic St. Mary's City Commission, pp. 54 (bottom), 106; Anne Arundel County's Lost Towns Project, p. 57 (top); Middlesex Registry of Deeds document courtesy of Virtual Jamestown, Virginia Center for Digital History, University of Virginia (www.virtualjamestown.org), p. 59; National Museum of Natural History, Smithsonian Institution in Washington, D.C./courtesy of Doug Owsley, staff photo, p. 65 (top left); *Portrait of Cecil Calvert*, a copy by Willem Wirtz after a copy by Florence McCubbin after the original by Gerard Soest. Historic St. Mary's City Commission, pp. 69 (top), 136 (bottom); Historic St. Mary's City Commission, photos by Henry Miller, pp. 69 (bottom), 71, 72, 76, 79 (top), 81 (both), 136 (third from top); National Museum of Natural History, Smithsonian Institution in Washington, D.C./courtesy of Doug Owsley, photo by Chip Clark, diagram from Historic St. Mary's City Commission, p. 73 (bottom); Historic St. Mary's City Commission, image by Mark Moore, p. 78; Huntingfield Collection, Maryland State Archives, MSA SC 1399-1-187, p. 105; © Claude E. Petrone, p. 110; © Sally Walker, p. 115; Maryland State Archives, General Assembly Upper House proceedings 1637-1658, Liber MC, folio 178, MSA S-977-1, 2/20/4/42, p. 118; © Paul Felix Photography/Alamy, p. 125; National Museum of Natural History, Smithsonian Institution in Washington, D.C./courtesy of Doug Owsley, photo by Dr. Bruno Frohlich, p. 127 (top right); National Museum of Natural History, Smithsonian Institution in Washington, D.C./courtesy of Doug Owsley, photos by Donald E. Hurlbert, pp. 127 (bottom), 128; Sculpture by StudioEIS, Brooklyn NY photo by BJ Ervick-StudiosEIS, pp. 129 (all), 130,137 (bottom); © iStockphoto.com/Phi2, (endpapers: wallpaper); © Photodisc/Getty Images, (endpapers: dirt).

Cover: National Museum of Natural History, Smithsonian Institution in Washington, D.C./courtesy of Doug Owsley, photos by Chip Clark, (front cover skeleton, bone texture on title and flaps, and back cover); © The Bridgeman Art Library/Getty Images, (map), © iStockphoto.com/Phi2, (back cover texture).